PRAISE FOR *The Art of Mingling*

"Ms. Martinet believes in mingling the way some people believe in yoga. To her it is a discipline and form of exercise to be practiced on a regular basis." *—The New York Times*

"Martinet has developed techniques for working any event with ease." *—Chicago Tribune*

"Jeanne Martinet has come to the rescue of wallflowers everywhere with *The Art of Mingling* . . . a book full of witty one-liners." *—Daily Mirror* (UK)

"Jeanne Martinet, author of *The Art of Mingling,* is an expert at navigating parties." *—New York Daily News*

"Jeanne Martinet's amusing guide contains nifty ideas designed to get the flower off the wall and into circulation."
—Letitia Baldridge

"If your idea of absolute terror is a room full of strangers at a party . . . then you'd benefit from *The Art of Mingling*."
—Single Life magazine

"Anyone who reads [*The Art of Mingling*] will end up being the belle of the ball. . . . I love it. I love it. I love it."
—Marjabelle Young Stewart

"*The Art of Mingling* takes the intimidation out of party scenes, whether they are business-related or social."

"Having all my life dreaded social mingling with an ever-increasing unease, I will now carry *The Art of Mingling* with me wherever I go, knowing I will no longer be at a loss for words."

Also by Jeanne Martinet

The Faux Pas Survival Guide

Getting Beyond Hello

Come-Ons, Comebacks, and Kiss-Offs

Artful Dodging

Truer Than True Romance

Life Is Friends

Etiquette for the End of the World

THE ART

of

MINGLING

Fun and Proven Techniques for

Mastering Any Room

JEANNE MARTINET

St. Martin's Griffin

New York

www.stmartins.com

The Library of Congress Cataloging-in-Publication Data is available upon request.

ISBN 978-1-250-06176-8 (trade paperback)
ISBN 978-1-4668-8018-4 (e-book)

Our books may be purchased in bulk for promotional, educational, or business use. Please contact your local bookseller or the Macmillan Corporate and Premium Sales Department at (800) 221-7945, extension 5442, or by e-mail at MacmillanSpecialMarkets@macmillan.com.

Revised Edition: October 2015

10 9 8 7 6 5 4 3 2 1

To Jason:

Best friend and ex-minglephobe

Acknowledgments

First of all, I am grateful to all the hostesses and hosts who ever invited me to a cocktail party or other social gathering. I really do wish I could name them all, as well as everyone who has ever given me a mingling tip or a great party story, but that would fill a separate book (or even two). If you are one of these people, please know how much I appreciate it. I am also forever beholden to my gregarious parents; those childhood summer band parties on our lawn and opera soirees in our club basement gave me my first taste for mingling.

Last but not least, a special thanks to everyone at St. Martin's Press, especially my supremely wonderful editor, Hannah Braaten.

Contents

Preface to the New Edition

Like all my best ideas, *The Art of Mingling* was born on a cock-tail napkin.

It happened in the wee hours of the morning after a wed-ding in Dayton, Ohio, while I was hanging out with college friends. We were performing a group postmortem on the re-ception, when suddenly my friend Larry said, almost accus-ingly, "Hey Jeanne, how did you manage to meet everyone in the entire town? The rest of us only talked to people we already knew." And so, more to entertain than to instruct, I proceeded to jot down on a napkin some of my favorite mingling tech-niques (which until that point in time I never knew I had names for) while I described their execution. To my amazement my friends were not only amused but actually seemed hungry for this information. That's when I realized that there were prob-ably a lot of other people eager to discover these time-tested mingling methods.

Still, when *The Art of Mingling* was first published in 1992 I was not completely aware of how much mingling-related fear existed out there. In identifying this pervasive social phobia and in offering my own personal system for socializing at parties, it seems I had struck a societal nerve. In fact, most of the people I talk to seem to want to learn how to become better, more confident minglers. Over the years even some TV talk-show hosts, radio personalities, and top executives have revealed to me that not only are they terrified of making small talk with strangers, but also that my lighthearted, down-to-earth approach appealed to them.

Unfortunately, in today's society our "mingling muscles" are becoming more and more atrophied, in part due to the enormous shift in the way we connect with each other. In the nine years since the last edition of this book, the now-iconic iPhone came into being, Twitter was created—and now has 271 million active users—and Facebook went from having 12 million users to over one billion. About 60 percent of U.S. adults now have smartphones; the average American spends about 11 hours a day with electronic media. The Internet is arguably the greatest people-connecting invention of our time, but are we really connecting? We can have conversations, business meetings, drinks, sex, or fights with people—all anonymously, and all online. But as far as face-to-face interaction goes, our aptitude is only decreasing.

For the last nine years I have been collecting brand-new mingling techniques, tips, and lines that I have incorporated into this updated edition in order to offer the reader more relevant social options and guidelines—such as the sections on the Secret of Listening, the Dumb Use of Smart Phones, and the

After-Party: Instructions for Following Up. Mingling methods may be the same as they ever were, but the accouterments—the menus and venues of minglers—are always changing. After all, there is a reason "temporary" is part of the word "contemporary."

I think most of us are aware that we need to keep improving the way in which we relate to each other as the world becomes more crowded, and more technologically advanced. *The Art of Mingling* started out as a humorous treatise on a subject I was passionate about, but by now it has become more or less my mission in life: to get people out there talking to each other— and by that I mostly mean talking to people they don't know (yet). Entering a room full of strangers is both wonderful and scary, like traveling to a foreign country. As with any other kind of exploration, it's always safer if you stay home, but remember: Nothing can be gained if you don't venture out into the unknown, and fewer things in life are more delicious than engaging, spontaneous conversation with someone new.

THE ART
of
MINGLING

Why Learn the Art of Mingling?

You are at a cocktail party. The guests are glamorous, the food is fabulous, the décor is divine—nothing could be more wonderful, right?

Wrong. It's a nightmare. You want desperately to disappear. Everywhere around you are people who seem to know each other. They are talking and laughing, having a great time, while you are standing all alone, wishing with all your heart and soul that you were somewhere else—anywhere else—but here. Two firm convictions keep you from dying on the spot: (1) You are definitely going to take the life of the friend who somehow convinced you that you needed to expand your horizons by coming to this party. And (2) If this night ever ends, you will *never ever* leave the safety of your home again.

An exaggeration? Maybe. But I know plenty of people, of all ages and from all walks of life, who are perfectly comfortable with one-on-one or small-group social interactions but confess to a secret terror of medium to large parties of any kind. The very *idea* of having to talk to a lot of people they don't know makes them go dry in the mouth. They'll do *anything* to avoid mingling situations. Many opt out, telling themselves they are skipping the party because they have too much to do at the office or that they are too tired to go—even that they have nothing to wear. Others, the self-diagnosed introverts of the world, tell themselves big parties are just "not their thing." This kind of avoidance is a shame bordering on a tragedy, because larger affairs, whether they be business or "social" functions, are potentially more exciting and energizing than small get-togethers. They are fertile arenas for meeting new and interesting people (I met a woman at a fund-raiser fifteen years ago who became one of my best friends). And yet, simply because of apprehension or aversion, people often waste these opportunities either by not going to the party, or by going with a colleague or companion and never leaving their side. Anything, they think, is better than to risk being left standing all alone looking pathetic. And even *that* is preferable to suffering the incomparable, utter agony of being face to face with a stranger and not knowing what to say.

People who feel this way (and there are more of them out there than you might imagine) have a widespread disease known as *minglephobia*. Is there a cure? Yes. Because contrary to what you might think, "making small talk," "being a social butterfly," or "working the room" is a learned art—a simple one—that *anyone* can master.

It's true that social skills seem to come more easily to some than others, and there are a lucky few who are actually born mingling geniuses (in fact, I once saw a small child work a room so well it was scary). But most people have to practice. With practice, even the pathologically shy, as well as the more common tongue-tied or foot-in-mouth types, can learn simple tricks, lines, and maneuvers that can mean the difference between misery and fun—between a night of feeling out of place and a night of feeling socially triumphant.

"Tricks? Lines?" some of you will undoubtedly protest. "But that sounds so insincere, so artificial." My response: There is a big difference between "artifice" and "art." If a dancer simply got up and did what came naturally, would that be as powerful and effective as when he performs practiced moves? Throughout this book I will suggest many small pretenses, but I will never encourage anyone to be untrue to themselves in any real sense. You must think of mingling as a kind of enjoyable and challenging game, like a tennis match. It's never a bad thing to learn a new skill. And after all, we are talking about mingling here, not marriage. It's about having fun.

Of course, there are a few misguided, non-minglephobic souls who think mingling takes too much energy or is simply a ridiculous waste of time, that it is nothing but an endless stream of meaningless conversations with people you will never see again. And yes, I admit I've had my share of inane discussions about weather or traffic. But I've also had countless ten-minute conversations about supposedly trivial subjects like wallpaper that were fascinating, after which I've usually gone home feeling buoyed and more connected to the world. You must never forget that simply being in a room full of people who are communicating with one another is exhilarating! Just look up "mingle" in the dictionary: "to become mixed, blended or united; to associate or mix in company." Sounds stimulating, even sexy, doesn't it? It is. I know from experience.

I'll tell you a secret. Although I have always adored parties—anywhere, anytime—mingling didn't come naturally to me at all. But when I was about thirteen, I made up my mind that I would become a mingling virtuoso. I proceeded to teach myself the art over the course of years, by trial and error. I have collected tips and adapted techniques from countless friends and acquaintances, as well as from books (mostly old ones, from previous eras when every well-brought-up person was highly proficient in the art of conversation). All the methods I use have been tested and honed for best results, and now I have a system that never fails. It's easy, and you can learn it, too.

Each of the following techniques and lines is applicable to just about any type of large gathering. However, there's one fundamental principle to remember as you begin to study this time-honored art: *Your purpose in any mingling situation is to have fun*. This is an absolutely vital, hard-and-fast rule; your success as a mingler depends on this basic premise. Whether you are at a business affair or a neighbor's party, whether you are mingling for love or for career advancement, your primary goal must be your own enjoyment. You may see a given mingling situation as a means to climbing the proverbial corporate ladder or hooking up with a hottie, but unless you truly enjoying meeting and talking with people, your success will be limited. The truth is that mingling is its own reward.

All of us have a deep desire for human connection. Conversation is one of life's greatest pleasures. The more people you meet and connect with, the more potential you have for happiness. Mingling can actually feed your spirit. In other words, the more you mingle, the better your life will be. The warm, communal feeling you will experience when you leave a party after meeting and enjoying new people will spread to the rest of your life, and enrich it. And trust me, if you become less socially fearful, you will be less fearful in other areas of your life—in your business life, in your relationships. The art of mingling may not be the answer to everything, but it is an important part of living a full and rewarding life.

So, take a deep breath, and *let's mingle*!

1

Overcoming Minglephobia

A WORD ABOUT WORLD WIDE WEB-HEADEDNESS

More and more, I hear this from people: "I don't need to go to parties to mingle. I'm having conversations every day with thousands of people. I mingle all the time. I have a rich and satisfying social life online. Why should I bother going to a party where I'll have less control over who I talk to? I have no interest in mixing it up with a bunch of boring strangers in person."

Listen. I get it. The social networking world is vast and dynamic and ultra-accessible. Why take the trouble to get dressed and go to a holiday party across town when you have movies or video games to stream, texting and tweeting to get to, and Seamless to order in your favorite takeout?

The thing is, twenty-five years ago, long before YouTube,

Facebook, Twitter, and Twitch, introverts were more in touch with their own minglephobia. When they were invited to a party where they would know few or none of the other guests, it was usually at least somewhat enticing to them. They would want to go but would be daunted by the prospect. It was too scary for them. Today, these very same people would profess that social networking is all the socializing they need, and that the Internet is a "great place to mingle."

Ahem. Let me make one thing perfectly clear to all you Digital Natives out there: *IM-ing is not mingling.* Emailing is not mingling; texting is not mingling; video chatting is not mingling; posting on Facebook and Twitter is not mingling. Mingling has not changed since the beginning of time: It's real people gathered in a real space together, conversing face to face (or, given the functionality of Facetime and Skype, perhaps I should say flesh to flesh). Socializing online is to real mingling what playing a Wii ski game is to actual skiing; the latter takes more effort and is riskier, sure, but so much more healthy, exhilarating, and rewarding. For one thing, at a real gathering there is a physical energy exchange between people. These subtleties of facial expression and body language are lost in cyberspace, as is the touch of someone's hand, or the shared experience of hearing the sound of laughter across the room.

Human beings crave connecting to other human beings the way they crave water or food. And as information technology pervades every aspect of our lives, we have more methods of communicating than we ever imagined possible. We can set up a webcam in our living rooms and millions of strangers can see us. We can trade messages instantly with people on the other side of the world. We can find the answer to just about anything at the touch of a button or the swipe of a screen. Who knows, someday we might be able to download hologram friends or use memory chips in our heads to communicate telepathically. But it still won't be "mingling" unless our corporeal bodies are in the same time/space continuum.

More and more, we find ourselves unwilling to make the commitment to talk to a real person who is right in front of us. I used to love talking to cabdrivers in New York City; I would learn something about their lives, and vice versa. Now every one of them is on his cell phone. And so guess what? So am I. I am not a Luddite. I am, in fact, addicted to my iPhone. For one thing, it helps me locate the party! And there is no question the Internet can be helpful for finding people with whom to mingle, and places in which to mingle.

The point is that before you can begin to cure a disease, you have to be aware you actually have one. A lot of people who are online all the time have minglephobia and don't even know it. If you have a friend or a family member who you believe is using texting, Facebook, Instagram, Gchat, and Twitter as a cover for his minglephobia, drag him to a cocktail party or an event at your local bar!

HOW TO FAKE IT TILL YOU MAKE IT

Okay. There you are, standing by yourself, frozen against the wall in a room full of people. You've just arrived, and you've already done the two things that made you look busy: taken off your coat and said hello to your host or hostess, who has long since dashed off to greet another guest or check on the ice supply. What now?

Number one (and numbers two and three): Don't panic. You are not the only person feeling this way. Many people descend into a state of almost existential angst when faced with tough mingling situations. Some people deal with their fears by immediately withdrawing into a dark corner, where they take out their cell phones and pretend to be engrossed in urgent communications. Some react by giggling when nothing is funny; some play with their hair or fiddle compulsively with their clothing. In fact, minglephobia can cause people to drink too much, eat too much, smoke too much, or—and this can really be dangerous—even dance too much! So it's important not to give in to your fears, especially in those first few crucial moments. Just try to relax and say to yourself, *"I'm going to fake it till I make it."*

Believe it or not, this simple affirmation is an effective, almost magical, way to transform party terror into a positive outlook. Remember when you were little and you and your friends told ghost stories to scare yourselves, and by the end of the night, you really did believe in ghosts? It was remarkably easy to fool yourself when you were a child, and it's just as easy to fool yourself as an adult. Just pretend to be happy to be wherever you are; make believe you are confident; simulate self-assurance—even for ten minutes—and an amazing thing will start to happen: You'll actually begin to feel that way, partially because of the response you receive from other people.

Many books have been written promoting the benefits of having a positive attitude—that it can attract people and other things you want in life. The question is, how do you muster that attitude when you are feeling intimidated and uncertain—and maybe more than a little scared? Let's face it. Very few people want to talk to someone who is showing outward signs of fear or depression (unless it's a party filled with out-of-work psychotherapists). So even though you will probably have at least some trepidation when approaching people you know little or not at all, you must practice putting it aside. Just as if you had to walk out on a stage. Deep breath. Curtain up. Before you know it, you'll discover you're no longer faking it; you'll find your fears have disappeared and you are actually having a good time!

Fake It Till You Make It is an attitude aid rather than a specific technique, but it's important to remember it as you begin to mingle, because it is the basis of all the opening gambits and entry lines. And of course I'm not asking you to "fake it" forever. Being totally phony is never a good idea. But your mindset as you enter the fray is extremely important. For the first few minutes of a difficult mingling experience, what you *project* is more important than what you may be feeling.

FOUR SURVIVAL FANTASIES FOR THE TRULY TERRIFIED

Sometimes the Fake It Till You Make It mantra isn't enough when you are faced with a room full of Serious Terror Inducers. Serious Terror Inducers are usually defined as people with whom you feel you have very little in common. The scariest groups for me are investment bankers, people at East Hampton art gallery openings, and the ladies' bridge club in Peoria, Illinois. But whether your own worst mingling nightmare is a singles' soiree, your company picnic, a high-pressure business affair, or just a neighborhood holiday cocktail party, the following survival fantasies can be lifesavers. They are for those times when you can hardly breathe, when you can't remember your name or the name of the person who invited you—or when you suddenly have no idea why you were even invited and suspect that someone's secretary must have made a horrible mistake in adding you to the guest list.

The need for this kind of psychological armor varies greatly, of course, with each individual and situation. Extraordinarily shy people or people who haven't been out of the house for two months may use the survival fantasies regularly. Some people (like me) find them to be so much fun that they use them occasionally for the pure kick they get out of them. But in any case, they can provide you with an instant shot of social confidence, enough to allow you to approach a group of intimidating strangers. All you need to make them work is a little imagination.

The Naked Room

Suppose you have just arrived at a large party. As you enter the room, you realize that (1) you don't know a soul there; (2) everyone is talking animatedly; and (3) the second you walked in, you lost every ounce of self-assurance you ever had.

Try this: Just for a moment, imagine that everyone in the room—except for you, of course—is wearing nothing but their underclothes (preferably plain or even raggedy in style; a Victoria Secret fantasy will not have the desired effect) and shoes. There are variations, naturally, according to what you think makes people look the most ridiculous and powerless;

some people prefer to visualize them in only socks, ties, and jewelry; in their pajamas; dressed as clowns; or even completely naked. You can try to imagine them all as four-year-olds. But whatever version works for you, the Naked Room fantasy can be an easy way to turn the tables when you're feeling vulnerable or exposed and is an excellent place to start to build your initial party confidence. In fact, strangers may be drawn to you by the amused smile on your face.

The Invisible Man

This fantasy is based on a very simple truth, something my mother used to tell me all the time: *Nobody is looking at you. Everyone is too busy worrying about themselves.* While this may not be 100 percent true, it is mostly true. The Invisible Man fantasy merely capitalizes on this basic fact, but takes it one step further. Ready? You're just *not there.* You don't exist. Do you think someone's looking at you, wondering snidely why no one is talking to you? You're wrong; they're looking right through you. They're looking at the food table, at the wall, at another guest. If you have ever seen the classic 1933 film *The Invisible Man,* there is a moment when Claude Rains takes off his bandages and is totally transparent. What power he has! How he laughs! Just like Harry Potter when he dons his invisibility cloak and is invincible. Now, "invisible" as you are, you are free to unselfconsciously walk around the room, looking at everyone, looking at the furniture, the paintings—the whole scene—with total relaxation. This gives you time to catch your breath, psychologically, until you feel ready to become visible again and enter the conversational clique of your choice. (Warning: The true introvert may want to be careful with this one; you don't want to stay invisible for too long. *Reappearance is an absolute must.*)

The Buddy System

Remember in elementary school when you went on field trips and your teacher made you line up with a partner so that no one would get lost? In my school, they called this the Buddy System. Well, here you are now, feeling psychologically "lost" in this room full of intimidating strangers. How can you possibly get up the nerve to speak to anyone?

Easy. You and your "best buddy" will go together. Tell yourself that just behind you, over your right shoulder, your very best friend in the whole world is moving with you through the room, listening to everything you say. Voilà: instant calm. After all, your friend loves you, right? Understands you? And probably will have a lot of the same opinions of the people you meet as you do. When you talk, you will be able to imagine this friend smiling at everything you say, offering encouragement and approval. If by chance you are snubbed by someone, you'll hear your friend whisper in your ear, "What an ass! Don't let it get to you; he's obviously really insecure. His loss!"

Of course, you mustn't get carried away and actually *speak* to your imaginary friend (at least, not so anyone can notice).

Celebrity Magic

This technique is kind of the Invisible Man fantasy in reverse. It may seem drastic to some readers, but I find it so effective, as well as so much fun, that I highly recommend it, especially for the more adventuresome. Don't forget, these fantasy techniques are specifically designed for *initial* courage—to get you to take that first step, to transform you from a guest with an inferiority complex into a participating, mingling member of the party. So try this: *Be someone else,* just for a little while. This might seem a bit radical, especially since other people have probably been telling you for decades to "be yourself," but if you're standing there at the party, terrified, halfway wishing you were somebody else anyway, then why not just do it? The person that you are is giving you a lot of trouble right now, and is obviously not the least bit happy about where it is. So pick a favorite celebrity, someone whose poise, posture, or personality you particularly admire, and then . . . slip into him or her. When done right, this technique works much faster than the other survival fantasies because of the mingling power most people attribute to stars—power that instantly becomes accessible to you.

I used to become Bette Davis, especially when faced with really tough rooms or if I were just feeling insecure for some reason. I would visualize her in one of her movie roles, like Margo Channing in *All About Eve,* and pretty soon I would sense my eyebrows going up slightly and my body relaxing as I surveyed the social battlefield with a truly languid amusement. As Bette Davis (or, more specifically, Davis in the role of Margo), I would not just be *ready* to mingle, I'd be positively *hungry* for it. No one, by the way, ever looked over at me and said, "Look at that weird woman pretending to be Bette Davis!" because no one, of course, ever noticed the difference. They merely saw a confident, perhaps even interesting, woman. Likewise, no one will be able to tell what *you* are doing when you use this technique. After all, that's why these are called "fantasies"—they're *secret.* Also, you don't have to use a celebrity. You can, if you want, pretend to be someone you know in real life, someone who is never ill at ease (or, more likely, who never *seems* to be ill at ease—they probably feel the same as you do inside, of course). The only guideline is that you must choose someone you know pretty well; the better you know this person, the easier it is to assume his or her persona.

Some useful celebrities for women: Lena Dunham, Amy Adams, Grace Kelly, Heidi Klum, Nicole Kidman, Lucy Liu, Natalie Portman, Katie Couric, Bette Davis, Angelina Jolie, Goldie Hawn, Katharine Hepburn, Scarlett Johansson, Vivien Leigh (as Scarlett, of course), Marilyn Monroe, Julia Roberts, Diane Sawyer, Oprah Winfrey, Reese Witherspoon, and Emma Stone. For men: Antonio Banderas, George Clooney, Johnny Depp, Jamie Foxx, Cary Grant, Jerry Seinfeld, Chris Rock, David Niven, David Sedaris, Jack Nicholson, Brad Pitt, Jon Stewart, Denzel Washington, and Anderson Cooper. Please note: It's best not to use people who are charismatic but may actually be frightening (like Christopher Walken or Ann Coulter).

Each of these survival fantasies will take some practice, particularly if you've never tried anything like this before. But believe me, they can help you, especially if you are a person who tends to freeze, to one degree or another, at the very beginning of a difficult mingling experience. You may also develop your own personalized survival fantasy, one that works better for you than any of the ones I have outlined, and that's fine, of course.

Now, bolstered by the survival fantasy of your choice, you

are ready to enter the ring, to approach a person or persons—to get to the actual "meat" of mingling.

CHOOSING YOUR FIRST CLIQUE

As in any game or art, deciding where to begin is very important. Every party, every large gathering, has its bright lights, its superstar mingle circles, its personality power points. Should you forge ahead and go right for the loudest, laughingest, most powerful enclave of people in the room?

Absolutely not! Not unless you consider yourself in the intermediate to advanced level in the art of mingling. After all, you've just gone through at least one survival fantasy to get you this far; you don't want to blow it now by getting shot down by the coolest guest at the party. First you need to get in some relatively safe practice.

Practice Your Mingle on a Wallflower

That's right. Scope out the most out-of-place-looking soul in the room. This will vary from party to party; it's all relative. Usually it's a quiet person standing alone, or two people who look a little lost, a little tentative. They may be inappropriately dressed, or at least not completely well put together. Lots of times you can identify this party misfit by his timid expression or shuffling stance, or by the way he appears fascinated by the photographs atop the piano. At any rate, you must think of this first person, or cluster of people (perhaps even several clusters, depending on how much practice you need), as your sketch pad, your scratch paper, your dress rehearsal. The PSAT of your mingling experience.

Keep in mind as you approach this person or group that one of your purposes here is to learn how certain kinds of conversation work, how they feel to you. Did introducing yourself come naturally to you, or did it sound stiff? Was a certain line or opening perhaps executed with the wrong inflection? In this way you can try out mingling techniques you'd ordinarily never dare to try. It's like practicing your swimming in the shallow end of the pool before venturing into the deep end. Of course, you must always remember, when you are "practicing your mingle" with the socially challenged, that the reaction you get is not necessarily the reaction you can expect from one of the party's brightest wits. Nevertheless, the opportunity to practice is invaluable for the minglephobe and should be taken advantage of whenever possible.

There is, as you might have guessed, an added benefit to this technique: Some of the most fascinating people in the world happen to be socially inhibited. While getting in some stress-free practice with your so-called wallflower, you may accidentally have the conversation of a lifetime.

Judging a Book by Its Cover

If you can't find any wallflowers to practice on, there is another very effective way to choose a safe and easy first mingling target. I learned this method while watching my father, a musician, at a rather stuffy benefit attended by mostly lawyers and bankers. He stood there sipping a drink and scoping out the party, not talking to anyone, for about fifteen minutes.

Typical Dad, I thought to myself, *totally antisocial.* Suddenly, he made a beeline for a man standing in the corner. Before long, the two of them were engrossed in conversation, laughing away. Curious, I joined them. ("Hey, Dad" is, by the way, always a good entrance line!) The "subject" my father had singled out was a journalist, and turned out to be rather a kindred spirit to my father. I noted that they talked on and off for the entire evening.

Later I asked my father how he had chosen this man to talk to, out of all the people at the party. "Easy," he replied. "He was the only man there without a suit and tie on." My father, who never wears a suit and tie if he can help it, had selected his first mingling subject on the basis of similar taste in clothes, on the assumption that the man's attire was an indication of a creative personality. And he was right!

Fact one: You can often tell a lot about a person by appearance. Fact two: It is almost always easier to converse with someone who is similar to you than with someone who is dissimilar (though it might not be as interesting). Therefore, if you choose a person who is dressed as you are, or even as you would *like* to be dressed, your chances of a comfortable, maybe even fun, exchange are increased. Because you are at the very beginning of your mingling and you're nervous, it's vital that your first couple of encounters go well, or you may give up and go home before you've even begun to mingle.

Body Language Check

If you were to enter a room where everyone was sitting down, the first thing you would do is look for an empty chair. In most mingling situations, you're going to be entering a room where everyone is standing (more or less), but you still need to find an open spot. Scrutinizing body language will help you find a person or group of people who will be receptive to talking to you.

I don't mean that you should stand around for a long time, analyzing your surroundings until you suddenly realize there is no food left and everyone has gone home. With a cursory scan you can fairly quickly ascertain which people are "open" and which are "closed." If you see three people in a tight circle who are laughing hysterically, or talking intently with their arms around each other, this is a closed group and will be difficult to enter. If, on the other hand, two people are standing loosely together, looking around the room with pleasant (though hopefully not vapid) expressions on their faces, this is an open situation. Most enclaves will fall somewhere in between these two extremes, of course. Take a quick inventory: Is there space between people's bodies? Is someone in the group looking out at the party population in general? Are they leaning in toward each other, as if they don't want anyone to overhear them? Trying to join two people who are talking earnestly to each other is riskiest; if their eyes never leave each other's faces you might take it as a DO NOT DISTURB sign.

Note: Don't forget about your own body language signals. Sometimes, especially when we're nervous, we are unaware of what we're physically projecting. If you keep your head up and your shoulders open and wide it will indicate that you are confident and ready to meet new people.

The Safety of Numbers

When making that all-important decision of whom to approach first, keep in mind one of the simplest, oldest maxims in the history of social interaction: *There is safety in numbers.* Whether you are making a gentle approach or a boisterously dramatic entrance, your chances of avoiding discomfiture are statistically better with a larger group of people. Either everyone will notice you as soon as you enter the circle—and because there are so many people some of them (at least one, anyhow) are bound to be polite—or no one will notice you joining the group, giving you ample time to listen, digest the different personalities, and choose an appropriate opening line—or escape from the clique totally unscathed, a virtual mingling virgin.

In general, the larger the group, the larger your range of options. Perhaps most important, in a large group you will almost definitely not die the horrible death of awkward silence, something that *can* happen when you are involved with a cluster of two or even three people.

Of course, the best defense against awkward silences is a great opening.

2

Open Sesame: Making a Successful Entrance

GET READY, GET SET . . .

You've selected a mingling target group and are ready to make your entrance. But wait—before we get to the specific openings, there are still a couple of things to consider.

To Shake or Not to Shake

This is not about how to stop trembling in fear. I'm talking about that age-old custom of hand-clasping, traditionally thought to be purely a matter of etiquette, and, in most business settings, as natural as breathing.

To tell the truth, I have found handshaking to be a precarious practice in many mingling situations. Often it interrupts any conversation that is already flowing among the circle of people you are entering, not to mention that people may be holding drinks, food, or other items—and there seem to be more and more people who are squeamish about shaking hands for sanitary reasons (logical or not). It also can punctuate, more loudly than you may want, the fact that you have officially joined the group. So, although most of us are trained by our parents that it is polite to shake hands with a person when first meeting them, my own rule for entering a group of more than two people is *not to shake* unless someone introduces himself or you are introduced to someone by a third person. There are exceptions to this directive; some approaches (the Honesty Approach, for example) or opening lines necessitate a handshake, and, of course, sometimes someone else initiates a handshake.

Men: This is going to be harder for you. For some reason, men love to shake hands, anytime, anywhere. Sew your hands to your pockets if you have to, but *don't stick out that hand unless someone else sticks his or hers out first.* (And please, people, no fist bumping introductions at cocktail parties. If I start seeing that on a regular basis, I swear I am going to turn in my Miss Mingle badge.)

About Your Smile

Needless to say, you should smile and make eye contact when meeting someone new. (Dogs wag their tails in greeting; humans smile.) But unless your approach involves the technique of abrupt interruption (see pages 27 and 112) I recommend that you use a subtle, closed-mouth smile until after you have had a verbal exchange. A toothy smile can seem too cheery; there is something decidedly off-putting, even odd, about a total stranger approaching you with an enormous grin on her face. It's distracting, to say the least, and makes the recipient wonder if he missed something or is being laughed at. On the other hand, a closed or toothless smile is polite, sophisticated, and more natural. Remember, you don't want to scare off the group you're joining! Plus, you want to save the full power of your smile for after the person has said something. Then a full, face-flooding smile can serve to bond you with the person, to make him or her feel liked and appreciated.

As usual, there are exceptions to this rule, but you'd probably know if you are one of them. For example, I know someone whose smile radiates personality anywhere he goes, and people actually gather around him just to warm themselves by his powerful pearly whites. He floats in and out of groups without following the closed-smile rule, without knowing the first thing about mingling, in fact. Obviously, if you have a nuclear smile like this, you should use it, teeth and all, as much as you want to (maybe even more than you want to!).

In any case, you shouldn't become self-conscious about your smile, as that can cause weird things to happen to your mouth. But if you would like to remember the rule about smiling, here's a little rhyme to memorize:

> *When going in,*
> *No toothful grin.*
> *Use, for a while,*
> *the closed-mouthed smile.*

The Philosophy of Fibbing: Why Some Lies Are Essential

Before we go any further it is important that I broach a touchy subject. Here it is: *You can't be a good mingler unless you are willing to lie a little.*

I am sometimes accused of being a sneaky, insincere sort of person, merely because some of my strategies and solutions happen to be based on the philanthropic fudging of the truth. These idealists—or rather, purists—believe that we would all be better off if everyone told the absolute truth all the time. I watched one of these "Honest Abes" in action at a barbecue in upstate New York one weekend. He was standing with me and a friend of mine when a woman approached, calling the Honest Abe by name. As the woman leaned forward for a greeting kiss, Abe put out his hand and said crisply, "I'd rather not kiss. Let's just shake hands."

The newcomer was visibly embarrassed. I was embarrassed *for* her. My friend was also embarrassed. We all stood there awkwardly while the proposed handshaking took place. The woman chatted with us for a minute but left as soon as she could. When she was gone I asked Abe just what the heck was going on between him and the would-be kisser. Abe told me that they were acquaintances, that there was nothing in particular between them. He went on to explain that he had been merely practicing his policy of total honesty. Apparently Abe didn't care for greeting kisses, and he was quite proud of his ability to clearly communicate his needs and feelings.

I had to bite my tongue (and believe me that's not a wise thing to do while you are eating spicy barbecue) to keep from asking Abe what had happened to his manners. Self-realization and personal integrity notwithstanding, how hard would it have been for Abe to have sacrificed his precious dedication to the truth just enough to add "I think I may be catching a cold" to his rebuff? Better yet, it would have been a fairly simple matter for him to have physically parried the kiss and just shaken the woman's hand without making any sort of confrontation out of it.

Too many people today pride themselves on being unequivocally truthful, when the greater truth is that the fabric of society is, and always has been, held together by an intricate weaving of gentle deceptions and subterfuges. Decades of self-improvement workshops, twelve-step programs, group therapy, and communication seminars have trained people to be more direct in expressing their feelings. But somewhere along the way we lost something very important, and honesty has become an overrated commodity. To wit: Too much truth is uncouth.

Please don't get me wrong. I *am* in favor of truth telling when it comes to couples counseling, court testimony, and tax returns. But when you have just been warmly greeted by a stranger at a party, you simply can*not* say: "Oh, I wasn't coming over to talk to you; it's just that you happen to be standing near the cheese plate." It all boils down to being kind, rather than honest.

Being willing and able to tell a white lie is in fact the cornerstone of the art of mingling, the basis from which most of the techniques in this book are taught. A little fibbing enables you to be in control of your social experience—to steer your own course through the party—and at the same time protect your fellow human beings from experiencing any embarrassment. Mingling is a dance that is enhanced by the use of tricky steps, and those steps usually involve good-natured, old-fashioned prevarication.

Among all civilized people a tacit agreement exists: When we are engaging in lighthearted socializing, not every word out of our mouths is gospel. Everyone expects a certain amount of white lying and, in most cases, even appreciates it. We just don't talk about it. (Well, okay, I do!)

THE FOUR BASIC ENTRANCE MANEUVERS

The Honest Approach

Fibbing is fun and effective, but if sincerity is more your style, there's always the Honest Approach.

After you've tried this and experienced the response, you'll be astonished at how few people follow this simple, straight-forward course of action. I first tried this opening on a wild impulse when I was feeling overwhelmingly lost at a very stuffy publication party for a prize-winning novelist. I didn't know a soul, and most of the guests were clustered in tight, closed groups of two or three—the hardest kind to enter smoothly. I slipped into a survival fantasy for a few moments, then marched right up to a pleasant-looking man who was totally engrossed in conversation. I stood beside him long enough for him to look over at me (maybe thirty or forty seconds, which can be a life-time in this situation) and then said, "Excuse me, I hope you don't mind my coming up to you out of the blue like this, but I don't know a single person here. I'm Jeanne Martinet . . ."

At the time, I thought it was a rather dangerous ploy. Imag-ine my delight when this fellow, whose name turned out to be Peter, smiled as if I had just handed him a million dollars and told me that he had always wanted to use that approach at a party but had always been too shy, that he thought it was great that I just introduced myself that way. We ended up having a long and enjoyable conversation. About a week after the party,

I actually received a letter from Peter, thanking me for re-minding him about an "important interpersonal skill." I have used the technique many times since then, and it has always worked, to varying degrees (though I never got any more fan mail about it!).

The honest approach works because it strikes a familiar chord in almost everyone, and because it immediately offers the power to the people you are approaching, creating a non-threatening situation. You have basically put yourself in their hands. The only trick is, you have to seem sincere. And to *seem* sincere, you have to *be* at least partially sincere. Therefore, it is best if you use this approach only when you truly don't know anyone at the event. The other thing to remember about the Honest Approach is that you should use it only once or twice at a specific party. If you use the line on anyone who has al-ready seen you talking animatedly to others at the party, you obviously lose credibility.

Note: This approach *is* one where it's okay, even helpful, to use a handshake. This is because it is *interruptive* in nature, and any blatant interruption is already so disruptive that a hand-shake will act as a communicative salve.

As with many mingling techniques, the Honest Approach will work best if tailored to suit your personality. But what-ever words you use, you're bound to have fun finding out that sometimes honesty really *is* the best policy.

The Fade-In

This thief-in-the-night gambit is usually too passive and too slow for my taste, but I know many people who absolutely swear by it. Move as inconspicuously as you can up to the circle of your choice. Listen carefully to everything that's being said as you draw near. (In other words, eavesdrop.) Your goal is to go unnoticed as you enter the enclave and to become an intrinsic part of it before anyone realizes you're a newcomer. If you pay close attention to the conversation while you are fading in, you'll be able to contribute to it at an appropriate place, as if you had been there all along, taking part in the discussion. If by chance you are discovered before your Fade-In is complete, you will, with any luck, have heard enough to make a pertinent comment and gain immediate acceptance.

The key to the Fade-In is acting as if you absolutely belong there, as if you have been an integral part of this group for hours, as if talking to this specific set of people is what you do for a living. You'll find it is incredibly easy to convince people just by acting as if something is true.

Warning: Be sure to complete your Fade-In. It's of vital importance that within a fairly short period of time, you either complete entry—that is, say something—or move on to another group. If you're insecure about meeting new people, your tendency will be to merely hang around the periphery, listening and not joining in. This is not mingling! Don't be a party ghost.

The Flattery Entrée

This opening is based on the premise that if you give someone positive energy, that's what you will get back in return. Almost everyone responds well to compliments, and there's no surer way to be sure of a welcome from a stranger. The method may seem self-explanatory, but there's a right way to flatter and a wrong way, especially in mingling situations. While everyone responds to certain kinds of flattery (complimenting people about their children or pets is a guaranteed win, for example), there are other kinds that can bomb in a nuclear way. Moreover, as you have presumably not met the person yet, you are limited in the types of compliments you can use as an opening line. Here are some Flattery Entrée Do's and Don'ts:

DON'T: Praise apparel or body shape
Opening Lines:
"Wow, that dress is exquisite!"
"Excuse me, but from the looks of you, you must be a cyclist or a runner."

To comment about someone's dress may seem like a good idea, especially if it's woman to woman, but remember, we are talking about an *opening* line. The main thing about flattery is that it's often better not to use it than to risk overkill. Unless someone is wearing a getup that is definitely meant to draw comments (and you'd better be sure about this), it's too personal to open with a remark about someone's clothing. To say you love someone's dress is basically the same as saying you like the way she looks—her figure, her style—and that's simply too forward for the Flattery Entrée. After you've talked to the person for a while, then you can use this line. Flattery in midmingle is a whole different matter.

As far as the cyclist line goes, any direct comments about a person's body, level of fitness, or attractiveness are taboo as opening lines, unless you are channeling Austin Powers.

DO: Praise accessories

Opening Lines:

"I love those earrings."

"Excuse me for interrupting but those are amazing eyeglasses. They're so cool!"

It's much more appropriate to comment on someone's accessories (earrings, scarves, eyeglasses, ties, pins, hats). It's a tribute to taste without being too personal. This is also a smart opening because you can follow it up by asking where the person got the item in question, and, depending on her answer ("A trip to China," "My boyfriend's mother," "I made them from stuff I found on the street"), you can get a good five or ten minutes' conversation out of it, especially if you're ready to let the response lead you off into exciting new territory! Warning: Make sure the person is actually *wearing* whatever it is before you use this line. You don't want to exclaim, "What a great hat!" only to discover it's not a hat but a toupee.

DON'T: Flatter the group by putting other people down

Opening Line:

"Hi. [speaking softly] Do you mind if I talk to you guys? I don't want to sound mean, but you're the only people here who seem at all interesting."

As mortifying as this is for me to admit, I once thought this might work in some crowds, and I'm always one for experimenting, so one New Year's Eve after too much champagne I tried it out. Boy, was I sorry. What a disaster! The two guys looked at me as if I were a bed bug, and while I was trying to figure out if there was something wrong with my delivery or what, I heard a sharp voice right behind me, where I thought no one was standing, say, "Thanks a lot!" Horror of horrors, someone else had overheard me. It took some pretty fancy footwork to recover. Anyway, even if you aren't overheard, this kind of thing is a bad idea for two reasons: (1) the people you are addressing may be good friends of other people at the party, and may therefore be insulted, and (2) it's simply too negative a comment for most people to accept as a compliment.

DO: Praise the group in a positive way
Opening Line:
"I heard the laughter from across the room. You all must be either very funny, or very happy, so I decided I'd come over and see if it might rub off on me!"

This is the kind of Flattery Entrée that can work really well (assuming you are approaching a circle of people who have really been laughing). It makes the people feel good without being threatening or too personal in any way, and it's believable, since you really can be drawn to people by their good energy. As with all openings, you will want to adapt it to your personality, using language that is comfortable for you.

DON'T: Use a compliment that is obviously insincere
Opening Line:
"Pardon me, you all seem like such nice people. Would you mind if I joined you?"

First of all, though this seems to smack of the Honest Approach, you can't possibly know these people are nice since you haven't talked to them yet; the comment will seem disingenuous. Second, this particular kind of line is too wimpy, too "gee whiz." A rapscallion in the group may rebuff you with "Well you're wrong, darlin'. We're all a terrible lot—you don't want to associate with us."

DO: Use a compliment that comes from the heart (or at least the general vicinity of the heart)

Opening Line:

"Pardon me, but I heard you are the person who made the stuffed mushrooms. I just wanted to tell you how delicious they are!"

If you try hard enough you can almost always find something that is both honest and complimentary. Part of being good at the Flattery Entrée is to become a keen observer at any gathering, whether it be a friend's cocktail party or a crowded waiting room. Look around for things that you admire. Ask the hostess to tell you about her guests' accomplishments so that you will have ammunition for the Flattery Entrée.

DON'T: Offer self-serving compliments

Opening Line:

"Bob told me that you and I have a lot in common, that, like me, you're also the life of the party!"

This is the kind of remark that only pretends to be about the other person; in reality it is the speaker who is singing his own praises. The whole point of the flattery entrée is to flatter others, not yourself.

DO: Offer self-deprecating compliments

Opening Line:

"I imagine you didn't have any trouble, but I have to say I was exhausted after walking up that big hill and then six flights of stairs."

This kind of flattery can be really effective, as it is unexpected and subtle, and makes the other person the winner in a comparison.

DON'T: Be a gusher

Opening Line:

"Oh my god! Are you the friend Annie told me just won the tennis tournament? Congratulations! Wow! I'm so thrilled I get to actually meet you in person! This is unbelievable!"

There is a difference between flattery and fawning. Don't go overboard. This kind of gushing is really only acceptable when among good friends, or if you are an oil well.

DO: Praise with finesse

Opening Line:

"Pardon me, but Annie told me you just won the tennis tournament. That's so impressive. Congratulations."

One note here: If you are going to congratulate someone on an accolade of some kind, have a follow-up question ready, for after the person thanks you. "How long have you been playing?" would work in the above example.

. . .

Always bear in mind that using flattery in an opening line and using it after you are involved in conversation are very different things. And with people you have met even once before, a whole world of "You look great!" and "Have you lost weight?" opens up to you. But while it's often true that "flattery will get you anywhere," until you get to know what kind of people you are dealing with, you have to be very careful with the butter.

The Sophistication Test

There's no better way to find out what kind of person you're talking to than this, and it's also an excellent icebreaker. I use the Sophistication Test often, especially when I'm feeling out of my element. It's a quick, surefire method of figuring out what kind of subject matter, what tone, and what level of familiarity is appropriate. Please note that this opener must be directed to only one or two people at a time; if you are entering a larger group, use the Test on one person in the group. The question that I've found works best is: *"So how did you get here?"* (Be sure to smile.)

This question can obviously be taken many different ways, which is the whole purpose of the Test. If the person answers "In a cab," you can relax a bit (although you might prepare to be a little bored); this person isn't going to throw you any curves and will probably stay more or less on the surface of things. If he or she replies "Well, I knew the hostess's ex-husband, so I guess that's how I rated," you know you've got a fun person with whom you can kid around somewhat. Even "How does anyone get anywhere?" is good news; it's a sign of a witty conversationalist. But watch out for the guy or gal who says "My father caught my mother on a good night"—this one's big trouble and you've got to really hold on to your proverbial hat.

There are only two other types of responses, and both of them call for immediate escape. One of them is "What business is it of yours?" and the other is "I have no idea." The former signifies overt hostility—almost always a hindrance to mingling—and the latter could be evidence of mental impairment of some kind (or heavy-duty drugs).

You may want to concoct your own Sophistication Test question or use one of the ones listed below, but be sure whoever you use it on hasn't heard you giving the same test to another guest. You don't want anyone to realize you are conducting preconversation research!

"So, what d'ya' think?"

"So, how do you fit into this picture?"

"Well, what's your role in all this?"

"How's it going?"

"What's your story?"

"What's your connection here?"

OPENING LINES FOR EVERY MOOD

If you choose not to use the Honest Approach, the Fade-In, the Flattery Entrée, or the Sophistication Test, you may want to employ one of the following opening lines. You also might think up some of your own lines to commit to memory. Most people can think of totally awesome opening lines—unfortunately, it's usually hours after the party has ended! If you prepare just a little, an opening line will roll off your tongue like magic. Just remember to follow a few simple rules:

1. **Never, never, never (trust me) use "What do you do for a living?" as an opening line.** It's not only unimaginative, it's dangerous. The person you are talking to may have just been fired, or have been out of work for two years. He may be a stay-at-home spouse. And even if he has a career, unless his job is something you find interesting or know something about, this opening can be a conversational dead end. Whether he's an insurance adjuster, a computer programmer, or a dishwasher, once the person's told you what he does for a living, you are bound by the rules of courtesy to stick around and chat with him about it. You can't very well say "Oh, sewage treatment, how fascinating," and then leave. This kind of opening also may come off as rude; it may seem to the person as if you are trying to find out right away how much money he makes and whether or not he is worth your time.

2. **Those who mingle best, mingle alone.** While you may have your *imaginary* "buddy" with you (if you're using the Buddy System), you don't want to actually mingle side by side with your mate or a friend—unless, of course, one of you knows most of the people there and is introducing the other one around. Occasionally you meet someone at the beginning of the party who is also a little minglephobic, and it's tempting to go around the room together the whole

night; after all, it seems less scary that way. This is a no-no. It's too hard to assimilate into clusters when you are a pair; it can be threatening and, at the same time, it just looks wussy.

3. **Whatever words are coming out of your mouth, say them with confidence.** If you find you're not getting anywhere with a certain line, but you can't understand why, try it one more time on someone else, perhaps with a different tone. If that doesn't work, then that particular line might not be right for you, or for the situation. But don't give up! Never forget, 90 percent of America has minglephobia, so you are not alone.

Here are some sample opening lines, listed in the order of the safest to the most daring.

Level One: Risk-Free

"This music reminds me of my childhood [high school days/college days]."

"So what was your day like today?"

"How do you know the host [hostess]?"

"Doesn't [name of host or hostess] look great tonight?"

"I just can't believe how [beautiful/dark/noisy/crowded/etc.] it is here, can you?"

"Isn't this [type of food you are eating or have tried] delicious?"

"I just love this place."

Level Two: Playful

"Am I interrupting something confidential?"

"Excuse me, but what is that wonderful-looking thing you're eating [drinking]?"

"Please tell me someone here is talking about their recent or upcoming vacation. I'm looking to relax vicariously."

"A little birdie told me this was the place to get the most up-to-date [name of your industry or professional area] news."

"I don't mean to interrupt . . . well, okay, I guess I do!"

"Hello! I'm practicing my mingling tonight. How am I doing?"

Level Three: Daring

"Okay guys, what's the password over here?"

"I don't know you and you don't know me. See how much we already have in common?"

"I've been told that I should come and talk to you. I can't tell you who told me; I'm sworn to secrecy."

"If you're who I think you are, I've just heard the most wonderful things about you!"

("If you're who I think you are, I've just heard the most terrible things about you.")

"If you promise not to ask about my job, I promise not to ask about yours."

"Excuse me, but my friend and I were talking about mingling techniques and she bet me I couldn't walk up to you and immediately start talking . . . please just smile—that's good—and talk to me so I can win fifty bucks."

"I'm tired of small talk. How about some big talk? Or at least medium."

Naturally, the success of these lines depends a lot on your delivery. Some of them require an ironic tone, some an exuberant smile, some an air of puzzlement. Some of them will suit you better than others. Select the ones that seem most like something you would say, and remember that you can always alter them to fit your own style. But don't be afraid to try something daring once in a while. It's not going to kill you, and it may *slay* them.

3

Now What? Tools and Rules for Continuing the Conversation

N ow that you've chosen your first target group and have bravely uttered your opening line, you may be wondering, "Now what? What happens after the opening?" Well, you've got three options:

1. You can hang about silently, listening to the other people in the group talk, satisfied that you've actually pulled off an opening and gotten in.
2. You can exit immediately upon completing the opening gambit, using one of the techniques described in Chapter 4.
3. You can segue smoothly into a conversation with one or more of the people with whom you are now standing.

Obviously, the most rewarding choice, from a mingling standpoint, is option 3, which is, for many people, the hardest part of the mingling experience. Getting into a group is one thing; holding your own in that group is another. Even a smashingly successful opening line is only the beginning, like getting accepted into college. Now you actually have to *go* to college. In fact, many people are just as terror-stricken after a successful opening line as they are after one that flubs, even though they presumably now have the other person's attention and everything is fine. A good response to your opening may give you a temporary high, but then your minglephobia usually sets in again. *Oh my god,* you think frantically to yourself, *What do I talk about with this person?* Don't worry. This chapter should give you enough ammunition so you won't end up tongue-tied ever again. It's much easier to find things to say than we have been conditioned to think. There's a whole world of subject matter out there, and there are some easy methods to keep a variety of topics at your fingertips.

But first of all, let's address the worst-case scenario.

RECOVERING FROM A FLUBBED OPENING

Sometimes your opening line will fall flat on the ground and just lie there, dead. Don't be disheartened; this can be demoralizing, but it happens to everyone at one time or another. There are things you can do:

- **Pretend it never happened.** Simply start over with another opening. For example, suppose you chose the Fade-In entrance, but you're noticed before you get a chance to listen to the conversation and complete the maneuver. Everyone has stopped talking and is looking at you. *Don't panic.* You can switch immediately to the Honest Approach, the Flattery Entrée, the Sophistication Test (this one's harder with a large group, but still doable), or deliver one of the opening lines you've memorized. It's really not difficult to move quickly to another opening gambit, and it's important to know that it is not unusual to use more than one opening. The essential thing is not to lose your confidence. Don't let it show that you are disappointed your opening missed its mark. The survival fantasies can really help at a time like this.

- **Be unapologetic.** Let's say you used the line "Am I interrupting something confidential?" and you get the number-one killer reaction from the group: They exchange looks with one another that say *What a weirdo!* and offer no verbal response of any kind. In other words, the Silent Treatment. Now, once in a while someone may respond to this particular line with a "Yes, actually you are," in which case you should apologize politely and move on, never to return. But in the case of the Silent Meanies, I suggest you laugh (if you can, or at least smile) and say, "I guess I did!" This indicates that you can't be intimidated and that you know you haven't done anything wrong. You've merely stumbled accidentally into a patch of boors.

- **Make something up.** In the same situation as above, for example, say, "Look, I know that sounded rather odd, but I just had the most unsettling experience; I introduced myself to some people over there, as [name of host] suggested, and they told me they were having a private conversation, *thank you very much,* and they didn't want to be disturbed. So I thought I'd better check this time!" Or, if you've approached someone from behind, you can always use the old standard, "Oh, excuse me! I really did think you were somebody else."

- **Be funny.** You definitely have to be careful with humor, which is something I'll address later in this chapter. But for some people, having their opening bomb is so devastating that the only way for them to keep up their confidence and go on is to strike back with a funny line, as a comedian does with hecklers. Take the same example of the "confidential" line and the worst-case, icy reaction. You might be able to win them with "Uh-oh, am I under arrest?" Or, how about "What? Has the stock market crashed?" If you are good at accents, you might even try "Pardonnez-moi. Vous ne parlez pas anglais? . . ."

- **Retreat.** If the response is really as hostile as the extreme case I've suggested, your best move may be just to leave these bozos in the dust, unless there's some pressing reason to try further (for example, if one of them happens to be an important business contact). Try someone else, and use a different line, at least for a while. Some lines are just wrong for some parties, and some lines may be ill-suited to you. Don't let one bad experience keep you from trying again.

CAREER TALK: YES OR NO?

Assuming your opening succeeds or that you recover your balance sufficiently after a flubbed opening, you're still going to need some ready topics for when the conversation lags or stops completely. (I don't want to frighten you, but the latter may happen if you're an inexperienced mingler.) Ideally, you want each interaction to last at least ten minutes—that's optimum mingle time—and usually the dialogue surrounding the opening will last no longer than one or two minutes. So what do you do when the fervor of the opening dies down, and the awkward cone of silence begins to descend?

Most people automatically leap right into "So what do you do for a living?" or more often, "What do *you* do?" as if occupations have already been the subject of much deliberation at the party.

Please believe me when I say that, unless you are at an event for your industry or profession, this is not a good idea. When and where to talk "career-ese" is a debatable issue, but I do not recommend it until and unless you have already established a rapport with the person(s). Many people disagree with me on this. After all, this advice goes against a golden rule of conversation that has been drilled into our heads, and that for the most part, serves us very well: People like it when you ask them to talk about themselves. This is, of course, basically true, and if you can't think of anything else, asking about someone's career certainly may be preferable to stuttering or fainting. In other words, it's a perfectly acceptable default position. But you should be aware of the possible consequences and pitfalls:

- The person's occupation may be something he **does not want to talk about**. It is, after all, a pretty personal question to ask a stranger. Maybe she came to the party to forget work. Maybe he hates his job. Or maybe, like me, she has a profession that will impede the normal flow of conversation. You'd be surprised what happens at parties when I tell people I make a living writing books about going to parties. It immediately seems to become the whole conversation, and everyone around me gets super self-conscious about their mingling skills. I sometimes tell people I am a ukulele player (which is in reality my hobby) just to avoid this phenomenon. Note: If someone asks you about your job and you don't really want to discuss it, you can use one of the subject changing techniques outlined in Chapter 5.

- The person's occupation may be something really **boring**, and something he or she just loves to talk about—for hours. This can be no fun at all, and makes you susceptible to what I call the "Glaze-Out," which is similar to being hypnotized, except that it's not relaxing or particularly good for you. It's almost impossible to mingle when you're in the grip of the Glaze-Out. When it happens to me, I find that I can't concentrate at all on what's being said (much less say anything myself except "Uh-huh") and I usually become transfixed by a small section of the person's face. On the other hand, I know a medical student who told me she once asked a man immediately upon meeting him what he did for a living, and when he answered "accountant" and began describing his job, she was so afraid she was going to reveal her boredom that she overcompensated by whooping out an enthusiastic "Wow!!

Really?!" She kept this up so long she ending up sleeping with him. (True story, I swear. I couldn't make that up.)

- The person's occupation may be something **repugnant** to you. He could be a proctologist, or a mortician, or a hair transplant technician, or a political operative from the *other* party, and what are you going to say then? A friend of mine who is a vegetarian told me about the time she introduced herself to an interesting-looking man at a large party and then right away asked him what he did.

  "I have my own butcher shop," he said, smiling proudly.

  "Oh . . . ah . . . I . . . how interesting," my friend managed to reply, blanching.

  "Yep. Best butcher in the city. In business for thirty-six years. And we're busier than ever . . ." He went on to describe in gruesome detail what his day had entailed, involving a delivery for the holidays: two dozen turduckens (turkeys stuffed with ducks stuffed with chickens) and some wild rabbit. "Say, what's the matter?" he asked after several minutes. "You look a little green."

  "Excuse me, won't you?" my friend finally squeaked. That was the end of that conversation. Her hasty exit would have been much less embarrassing if she had talked to the man a little longer before she brought up professions. As it was, it seemed as if she introduced herself and then immediately bolted. Remember, when you ask this question you have no idea what subject you are bringing up!

- The person's occupation may be something **depressing** (or embarrassing). Let's say you've used flattery as your entrance.

You're all smiles and cheer from delivering the compliment, and then you ask "What do you do?" Suppose the person says with a quiver in his or her lip, "Well, actually, I'm between jobs at the moment, and I, well, today I thought I had gotten this job but . . . I didn't." This isn't a total disaster, of course, but it's not the greatest thing in the world to work with, as you almost have to come back with, "Oh, I'm sorry to hear that. What field are you in?" and you're going to have some real downer minutes before you can change the subject. The answer could also be something that's depressing to *you*. The person could work with drug-addicted babies, and while that is a compelling subject and a noble job, you might not want to find yourself in that kind of conversation right off the bat.

The point is, you are playing conversational roulette with the career query, and it could leave you in the position of wanting out desperately, before you've said more than two sentences. And beware: *The sooner it is after you have started the conversation, the harder it is to escape.* Also, if you pose this question to more than one person, it often means the destruction of the group as a unit. One person answers, and because of the nature of the dialogue, some or all of the others can use your entrance into this subject to escape, which they will do, especially if they've already discovered the person is a snooze. Now you're really stuck, because it is much harder to escape from one person than from many. At the very least, you've lessened your chances of having witty repartee or a back-and-forth among the whole group you've just taken great pains to enter. So before you jump into career talk, find out a little more about this person (or people) first. Note: The Sophistication Test sometimes works even better as a second line than it does as a first.

If you *must* talk careers right away, try a career semi-query. For instance, say, "Did you come here directly from work?" That way, it opens up the field for career talk, but you have a little safety zone to protect yourself in case something dreadful happens.

As far as career talk goes, there are more exceptions to this rule than in any other area of mingling. For one thing, none of these warnings apply if you are at a specific business function, such as a company party or your industry's convention. Also, there are many situations in which you can tell right away, for a wide variety of reasons, that it is a safe question and one you are expected to ask. It's certainly not the worst thing you can do, by any means. I'm merely urging you to remember the dangers and consider other options before you commit to this. There's so much more to talk about, so many other ways to enjoy mingling.

TEN TRIED-AND-TRUE TRICKS OF THE TRADE

A Mnemonic for Those at a Loss for Words

So what *do* you talk about when you're standing there with nothing but a blank computer screen in your mind, and you can't seem to find the button to make anything appear? We've all been in this position, where ten seconds of silence can seem like an hour. Even though you are probably not alone in your terror—as obviously no one else in your group is saying anything either—if *you* approached *them,* it is *your* responsibility to get things going.

We all know there are literally millions of subjects from which to choose: questions about the person's background or connection to the host or hostess; observations about the party or about current events; and, if it's a business affair, remarks about whatever may be new or exciting in your profession. The problem is how to pull something out of the air when you're stumped. So before we go any further, I'm going to offer you a very simple way—a fun trick, really—to think of a topic.

When you were a child, did you ever memorize things by using word-association games? I can still remember listening to my mother coaching my brother with, "What's the capital of Maryland? It's such a *merry land* that everyone in it gets *an apple.* Annapolis!" Sound silly? Maybe, but it worked, and while this kind of mental trick might not suit everyone, you'll never draw a blank again if you can learn to use the following memory aide for the subject-starved minglephobic.

Ready? After you have completed your opening, if the evil fog of silence starts to engulf you, all you need to do is to think *M.I.N.G.L.E.,* and use the initials to remind you of these all-purpose topics:

"**M**" stands for **Meeting.** (As in: "It's so nice to meet new people." "So lovely to meet so many of [name of host]'s friends!" "I feel as though we've met before. Have we?" Or, "Where did you first meet the hostess?")

"**I**" stands for **Internet.** (As in: "So, how many baby-yodeling videos [or whatever the current meme may be] have you seen today? Is it ever going to stop?" "Did you see that piece about the recent bitcoin scam that was trending on Twitter?" "I just heard that Amazon bought another start-up for a billion dollars!" Or, "Has anyone here had trouble getting on the Internet today or is it just me?")

"N" stands for **Nearby places.** (As in, "I envy [name of host] for living so close to [name of restaurant]." "I haven't been to this area for a while. I can't believe how much it has changed/hasn't changed." Or, "Did you notice that huge new building being built half a block from here?")

"G" stands for **Go.** ("Do you go to a lot of these parties?" "Are you going away for the holidays?" "Are you going to the morning conference meeting [hospitality suite] tomorrow?" Or, "I don't often go to big parties held at bars, but this is really fun.")

"L" stands for **Likes and dislikes.** (As in "I really like this cheese." "I love it when Janet has these parties!" Or, "I hate being so late, what did I miss?")

"E" stands for **Events.** (As in "Have you been following the Olympics?" "Did you hear whether they got those workers out of that coal mine?" Or, "Have you been to see the Matisse show that's at the museum now? I heard it's fantastic.")

Please note: As always, the sample lines I've provided are merely examples. You can adapt the topics to your own sensibility, of course. Or you may prefer to substitute some of your own topics—ones that are easily accessible to you.

Also, I've found it's best to stick with observations, or questions of a fairly nonpersonal nature, at least at the beginning of a conversation. This is because they are less threatening and because, for the best mingling experience, you need to remain in control so that you will be able to move off to another person or group should you feel like it. Specific questions about someone's life, while easy for most people to think of, usually commit you to a lengthy discourse with one person in the group. Remember, it is not called "small talk" for nothing. Ideally, mingling conversation should feel like playing. Using a little imagination will pay off in the long run!

The Interview

There are, of course, many who maintain that the formula for social success is simply to ask a lot of questions of the other person. Unquestionably, showing curiosity about others is the golden rule of all interaction; no matter how many tricks you learn, nothing will work if you are not interested in other people. It is, however, an oversimplification to say that all you have to do is ask questions. (If it were that easy there wouldn't be so many blogs and articles about how to talk to people, and you wouldn't be reading this book!) For one thing, exactly what questions are you supposed to ask a stranger? Most people can't come up with anything when they are nervous, and it can be hard to know what kinds of things are too intrusive to ask and what kinds aren't.

More important, merely asking questions may not result in the give-and-take that is essential to lively conversation. Obviously, a willingness to listen to the other person is a virtue;

yet, ultimately, conversations when you are mingling should be like a volleyball game, with everyone participating equally. For some people, interviewing can actually be a hiding technique: If you continue asking the other person about himself, you never have to share anything about yourself. In addition, the interview technique can upset the integrity of a group, because you can only interview one person at a time. If you walk up to Sharon and Emily, and start interviewing Sharon, Emily will quickly go elsewhere.

Given the above provisos, interviewing someone can still be a perfectly fine way to proceed. If you are standing with only one person, and it's what comes naturally to you, feel free to conduct an interview. Especially when you find yourself faced with a very shy person, the interview style is sometimes the only way to draw him out. (And perhaps, at some point, the other person will turn the tables and interview *you* after a while.)

So go ahead: Pretend you're Barbara Walters, Jimmy Fallon, or Terry Gross. Ask lots of questions—preferably questions that require more than a yes or no answer. (I do *not* recommend you use the Charlie Rose style of interviewing—that is, asking questions that go on and on until neither one of you can remember where you began!) Start with asking what connection the person has to the event and let his answer lead you to the next question.

Try to have your next question ready as soon as his reply is out of his mouth; his answers might not be lengthy. If he's a minglephobe, he may reply with a simple "Yes, I am." Or a "No, I didn't." As you ask the questions, watch his face carefully for any signs of life. If you see a flicker, you may have hit upon a conversational hot spot, and you will want to pursue that line of questioning.

The best interviewer will be able to counter any reticence on the interviewee's part by couching the questions in examples, and in that way inspire the interviewee to embellish his answers. This will create a richer conversation that is more of an authentic back-and-forth. For example, you might say, upon finding out that the person has just moved into a new apartment or house, "The last time I moved was ten years ago, when I moved to the financial district. It took me a while to get comfortable with the neighborhood—find the best coffee, the best takeout pizza, the best dry cleaners, and the best neighborhood restaurants. And I really missed this wonderful mom-and-pop hardware store we had before. How's the move been for you so far?" If you do this well, you may find the interview transformed into a rich, rewarding exchange.

Playing a Game

Here's a really fun way to keep things going. It takes a little courage, but you'll be pleasantly surprised at how well most people respond. I use this technique quite often, though I never realized it until several years ago, when I was spending a weekend with a friend in Stockbridge, Massachusetts. He and I had been arguing good-naturedly all day about whether my jacket was orange or red (he thought it was red; I thought it was orange). That night we went to a pig roast where I knew no one. My friend immediately melted into the crowd, leaving me to fend for myself. Never being one to stand alone in a corner, I marched right up to a group of people and entered it, using the

Honest Approach. After the introductions were finished, there was that inevitable moment of silence; my entry had disturbed the conversational flow.

Suddenly I had an idea. As if it were plaguing my mind, I asked the group at large, "What color would you call this jacket?" They were a little taken aback, but intrigued. They each answered in turn, and I noted that the two guys said "red," and the woman, "orange." This led to a quite interesting conversation about color perception and sex differences, and, as anyone knows, once you start talking about the differences between the sexes, you're home free.

The great thing about Playing a Game is it is such a fluid mingling technique. It facilitates bringing new members into the group ("Hey, come over here, we want to ask you something!") as well as exiting a group ("I'll be back, I want some other opinions!"). Also, you get to know people by how they play the game, which is a more relaxing, easier—and sometimes more revealing—way to find out about someone. Game playing is one of my absolutely most recommended tactics; it epitomizes the true spirit of mingling.

Here are some sample game lines to explore. However, you'll definitely discover that, after you've used this device once or twice, you will begin to invent your own. Don't ever forget your primary goal (even if you are at a business function): Have fun!

"What color would you say this [_____] is?"

What is that you're drinking? Wait, let me guess."

"I'm fascinated by regional accents. Let me guess where you grew up." ["Can you guess where I'm from?"]

"Close your eyes. Now tell me what I'm wearing [what color eyes I have]."

"Tell me three things about your company and I'll guess what company it is."

"My friend and I are having a disagreement, so I'm taking a poll. What do you guys think: Is kissing cheating?"

Room with a View

If you are at a fairly large party, you might want to try using this strategy, which is low risk but still marvelously effective. This is especially useful for those times when you are feeling very non-witty, and you have just begun to talk to either one or two people (it works best in a small group).

What you do is point out (discreetly, please!) someone else at the party, preferably someone across the room, and make an observation. Everyone loves to talk about other people, and this way you can have a very nonthreatening verbal exchange and find out a little about the person you're talking to before you decide to enter into more personal territory. Here are some lines you might try:

"Did you see that woman by the bar? Isn't that the wildest hat you've ever seen?"

"Just look at Andrew. I've never seen him look so happy."

"See that woman over by the door? Do you know who she is? I think I've met her somewhere, but I can't remember."

"Is that Joyce's son? He's so tall now."

"Have you talked to that person over there? Is she a friend of yours? I found her very interesting [funny, mysterious, etc.]."

The lines you use, of course, will depend on what you can notice about people at a specific party. If you're at a Halloween party you can have a field day! Warning: I am not condoning vicious gossip. It is vital to remember that you are not, under any circumstances, to say anything nasty about the object of your voyeurism. Doing so can get you into more hot water than I have space to talk about here.

Using Clichés

As I writer I know they are supposed to be verboten, but I can't help it: I love clichés—they are like old songs that make you feel good because you can sing along. However, just because I am overly fond of clichés myself doesn't mean that I necessarily advocate their use for others. But I do believe there is a good way, in conversations, to use clichés effectively.

Irony is the key. The following lines, executed with enough irony, sarcasm, or just plain whimsy, can become your staples:

"Haven't I seen you somewhere before?"

"Come here often?"

"What's a nice girl like you doing in a place like this?"

"What's your sign?"

"We've got to stop meeting like this."

When exaggerated, these dusty old standards can work as openers or as second or third lines (in fact, better irony results if they are *not* first lines), and they also serve as a sort of Sophistication Test. Best of all, they're easy to remember!

About Eye Contact

When it comes to being a good mingler, subject matter isn't everything. The wittiest line, if it's delivered while you're looking at the floor or someone's crotch, is worthless. In fact, many people believe that what you are doing with your eyes during a conversation is just as important as what you are saying. Here are a few tried-and-true tips about how your eyes, the most important mingling asset you possess, should behave.

- **Always look straight at anyone who is speaking to you.** I mean this literally; look into the person's eyes during those times when sound is actually coming out of that person's mouth. Eyes are extremely powerful, and as long as you are looking at the other person, you can be in La-La Land and still appear to be listening. Of course, you should always make an effort to be a good listener (see page 70), but at the very least, you should never reveal to the other person that you are not listening to every word.

- **Use the time when you are the one speaking to look away.** Certainly, if you are having a very intense discussion, you may be too riveted to want to do this, and that's great. But it's a principle of human communication that while you are speaking, you can turn your eyes anywhere else in the room and still seem totally involved in your conversation. People's eyes tend to move around when they are thinking. Therefore your eye wandering is okay as long as, when the other person resumes speaking, you immediately make eye contact with them again. This really works, although it seems to surprise people whenever I mention it. The important thing is that you do not appear to be scanning the room, which would obviously be impolite. Note: With close friends, the rules of eye contact change. Both people can stare at a table lamp and it doesn't matter.

  I encourage you to practice your eye roaming, because it is essential, if you want to become an expert mingler, to be aware of what is happening around you. First, your escape will be a lot easier if you know where you want to escape to. Second, there are techniques you may want to slide into at a moment's notice—a Room with a View, the Human Sacrifice—that necessitate keen peripheral vision. Again, I am *not* suggesting that you stop listening to the person you are talking to. We are talking about an occasional, subtle surveying.

- **Use your eyes for emphasis.** If you learn to use your eyes well, it's almost as good as having a million-dollar smile. Many people, in their frenzy to keep up a dialogue, forget that the eyes are the true center of communication. You can use eye contact to pick someone out of a group and let him know you want to talk to him one-on-one. You can use your eyes, along with a very slight nod, to point out something in the room. You can use eye expressions instead of words, either because words fail you or just because your eyes can say it better: roll your eyes ("Oh, I *know*!"); shut your eyes (Oh, how horrible!"); blink your eyes fast ("I'm trying to take this in, but it's all very strange"); or raise your eyebrows ("Oh, really?"). I happen to be one of those people who can raise one eyebrow, a dramatic gesture that can be quite effective (Oh, *come on* now!"). Eye expressions can not only save you when you don't know what to say, but also add to your general conversational charm.

The Dot-Dot-Dot Plot

This is one of those tricks it's hard to talk about. No one likes to admit they are sometimes so bored by other people, or so distracted by their own inner thoughts, that they zone out and lose the thread of the conversation. This can be *very* awkward at a party. The panic you feel when you "come to" in this situation is exactly like getting called on in class when you've been daydreaming.

The truth is I find the Dot-Dot-Dot Plot a useful technique because—I am somewhat embarrassed to confess—if someone starts describing in painstaking and seemingly never-ending detail her search for the perfect pastel place mats for her perfect pastel summer house, my mind is apt to wander. Suddenly I'll realize with horror I have no idea what the woman has just been saying. And now she's finally *stopped* talking and I am expected to respond.

Even if you happen to be better at staying focused than I am, you will invariably get caught in this situation every once in a while, if only because the hot roast beef or a hot guy just caught your eye for a moment and distracted you. Getting caught not paying attention at a party when someone is speaking directly to you is a *serious* mingling faux pas. I still experience that split-second rush of adrenaline when it happens. But then I remember: Have no fear, the Dot-Dot-Dot Plot is here!

When you "come to" in this situation, you almost always are aware of the last few words the person has said. It's just that without any other clues, you're lost. What you can do is use those few words any way you can, and then employ the all-important, all-powerful pause. She is not going to suspect you haven't been listening (unless you tell her) if you *have maintained eye contact,* per the instructions above. Keep in mind that other people are busy thinking about how well they themselves are communicating. So as long as you give them a "So then you . . . ?" "You mean . . . ," or "Wow . . ." they'll go right on talking.

I promise that you are going to be surprised at how well this works. It's scary the first time you try it; it sort of feels like stepping off the edge of a cliff, but when you find out how successful and powerful the pause is, you'll be astounded. One of the most popular closing techniques taught at sales seminars is something called the "Pause Close." It's based on the same principle as the Dot-Dot-Dot Plot: Human beings are very uncomfortable with pauses and will automatically do anything to end them. The Dot-Dot-Dot Plot is really very simple to use; in a way, it is just a glorified version of "Uh-huh." Note: The more you are able to work the last few words you may have heard into your delivery, the more convincing it will be.

If you employ one of the coaxing phrases below, and no one ever finds out you hadn't been paying attention, start listening with all your might. The Dot-Dot-Dot Plot is like a superhero weapon that can only fire once.

"So then you . . ."

"You mean . . ."

"Wow . . ."

"So what you're saying is . . ."

"Hmm. I don't know much about that kind of thing . . ."

"You can say that again . . ."

"You're kidding . . . really?"

"You can't be serious . . ."

"That's so cool . . ."

"I love hearing that kind of thing . . ."

"Then what happened?"

The Echo Chamber

A close cousin to the Dot-Dot-Dot Plot, the Echo Chamber is not particularly inspired or witty, but it is a great contingency strategy. It is for those times when you are completely aware of what is being said to you, but for some reason your social machinery is on the blink. Use this technique when you are very tired or suffering from general brain freeze. It's a bit of an inane way to converse, so it's best to use it just for resting, like putting the controls of the plane on automatic pilot temporarily. Here's an example:

OTHER PERSON: ". . . So, I told Susie she had to choose: soccer or the school play."

YOU: "Right. Soccer or the school play."

OTHER PERSON: "But her best friend Harriet is doing both. So now of course Susie thinks *she* should be able to do both. It's a mess."

YOU: "God, you're right. What a mess."

OTHER PERSON: "But you know, she has to learn that just because the other kids get to do something, that doesn't mean she does. Life doesn't work that way."

YOU: "That's for sure. Life doesn't work that way."

Okay, so it's not an earth-shattering exchange. But remember, this is a fallback tactic, meant for temporary use only. Note: It helps to smile and/or laugh during the Echo Chamber. Otherwise people will suspect you are not really participating in the conversation.

The Funny Thing About Humor

The funny thing about humor is how often people try to be funny and how rarely they are. A lot of people see a bright, gaily laughing group and think laughter must be the key to success, and therefore they've got to be funny. But there's nothing worse than humor badly executed while mingling. Don't let this happen to you:

"Wanna hear a funny story? Ha Ha! This is so funny, it's going to kill you! A man walks up to a . . . this is so funny, just wait . . . a man walks up to a bar . . . ha ha . . . I mean, a woman walks up to a bar, no a woman walks *into* a bar, hee hee, no . . . this is so great, you'll love it, you're going to LOL, wait . . . hey, wait a minute, where are you going?"

This is an extreme case, of course, but you'd be surprised how many people turn to humor when they shouldn't—especially when they are nervous. When a joke works, the rewards are great; when it doesn't, it's a disaster. Humor is very subjective, and its success or failure depends as much on the audience as grape vines do on the climate. And as Dorothy Parker once said, "There's a hell of a difference between wise-cracking and wit. Wit has truth in it; wise-cracking is simply calisthenics with words." I'm not about to try to teach anyone how to be witty. But here are a few basic guidelines:

- **Don't try too hard to be funny.** If you're trying too hard, it probably won't be funny. Be aware that you may overreach when you are feeling insecure.
- **Don't tell jokes.** Unless you enter a group that is already telling jokes, or the joke you have to tell is a proven success *and* is relevant to the situation (the

day's events, the party itself, etc.), it is best to stay away from joke telling. There are few things worse than when your joke bombs in front of strangers (ask any comic).

- **Don't announce in advance that your personal anecdote is going to be funny.**
- **Don't make your stories inordinately long.**
- **Don't touch people to encourage them to laugh.** It's as if you are saying to the person, "Hey, did you hear me, did you get it?"
- **Don't laugh too much yourself.** In fact, it's best not to laugh at all, at least not until they do. A big smile is enough.
- **Don't make fun of other people.** If you must make fun of someone to get a laugh, let it be yourself.
- **Don't make off-color remarks.** Humor of a sexual or crude nature should be avoided unless you're with people you know *very* well.
- **Don't be a punster.** Many people disdain puns. Example: "I used to be a banker but I lost interest." If you can't manage to hold back a pun, be prepared for rolling eyes. On the other hand, I sometimes like to use puns (in case you hadn't noticed) while self-consciously anticipating the groans—as if to say: "I know, I know, isn't that wonderfully horrible?"

How to Handle the Joker in Every Deck

As you know, there's usually one humor nitwit at every party. Besides escape, which is the subject of the next chapter, there are a couple of defensive techniques that will help. If it's a joke-telling joker, you can always say, "Oh, yes, that's a funny one, but I'm afraid I've heard it already," either to shut him up or to explain why you're not laughing. Or before they can get going, smile politely and say, "I have to warn you I'm not really a joke person."

Let's say you are up against someone who seems to thrive on saying stupid things and then laughing at them. If you choose to stay in the vicinity of this person or for some reason cannot escape, you're going to have to decide whether to humor the idiot or try to squelch him. You can always try "It's good to see you can crack yourself up like that." Or just smile vaguely until he gets the point that you don't think he's funny. In the end, we have to forgive even the worst jokers. They mean well, after all, and may simply be unsure of themselves, so always try to be kind.

TO BEMOAN OR NOT TO BEMOAN

It's happened to everyone at one time or another: You arrive at the party in a totally vile mood. Whether it's because you're stressed to the max or you're so blue you feel like a bad bruise, you can't imagine making small talk. You don't feel like forcing a smile, and you are completely dreading the question "How are you?" because you are very much afraid you are going to answer with the truth, and the truth is, "Horrible." You know this is not acceptable. Negativity, like dirty laundry, is something we all have but are supposed to keep tucked safely away at social events. "Laugh and the world laughs with you; cry and you cry alone" as the saying goes.

But is this true? Do you always have to put on a happy face, or can you—do you dare to—tell people how you really feel? Is there an acceptable way to reveal your sorry state of mind, providing you don't spend the entire conversation complaining?

Obviously, if you have friends at the party you can mention your lousy mood—after all, what are friends for? But even if you are in a room full of strangers, some of those strangers may be able to relate to your emotional state. I believe that if you are careful about it, sharing your foul mood can actually be an effective way of bonding with someone, if you follow a few simple guidelines:

1. Never give in to the temptation to try to "one-down" a fellow sufferer. When you discover a kindred complainer, often the inclination is for you both to start comparing notes about your bad experiences. For some people, complaining is a competitive sport, but you really don't want to get into a "Who is more miserable" contest. For example, I overheard a version of the following conversation once at a party on the Upper East Side of Manhattan:

    MAN ONE: "How are you?"
    MAN TWO: "It's been a little tough. You?"
    MAN ONE: "Horrible. The last two quarters have been a nightmare and they're cutting our benefits again."
    MAN TWO: "It could be worse. I lost my job nine months ago and I'm just about to lose my company insurance altogether."
    MAN ONE: "Wow, sorry to hear that. Well, at least you don't have that terrible commute to New Jersey

anymore. I've had to go there every weekend to visit my sick father, and because of all the construction the traffic is murder."

MAN TWO: "I only *wish* my relatives were in New Jersey. I've been traveling to Philadelphia to take care of my mother-in-law. Try that for a couple of months!"

MAN ONE: "That's rough, man. Anyway I gotta run. I should have been home ten minutes ago.

MAN TWO: "Ten minutes! I was supposed to be home *two hours* ago!"

(I know I have been telling you throughout this book that mingling should be like a game; however, a conversation like this one is more like a blood sport, which is not much fun.)

2. Try not to transmit your negative vibe to anyone. Negative energy transference between people occurs all the time, in public, at the office, at home—and at parties. In your current bad mood you are potentially contagious, as if you have the flu. Just as we should cover our mouths when we cough we must endeavor to avoid spreading social "dis-ease" when we are feeling low. What this means is that if you make a remark about how bad your day was, and the other person seems unsympathetic, or uncomfortable, suck it up and immediately switch into Fake It Till You Make It mode.

3. If at all possible, use humor and warmth when complaining. In other words, you have to make the other people understand that you may be sharing how you feel, but you

are in no way blaming either them or the party. Your underlying message should be that meeting them is the opposite of a bad thing. Revealing your inner gloom always needs to be done with some charm.

Here's a little quiz for those times when you find yourself mingling under your own personal black cloud and someone asks "How are you?" Should you or should you not use the following lines? Let's see how you do:

Line: *"Well, not counting today, I'm pretty good. How are you?"*
(YES. This may not be entirely true, as you may not be "pretty good" in any way you can possibly imagine, but it does acknowledge your current frustration, so you won't have to completely hide your bad mood.)

Line: *"Life pretty much sucks for most people right now, wouldn't you agree?"*
(NO. This line pretends to be about something other than just you, but it presents a negative world view—much bigger than having a bad day—and you might as well paste a big "L" for loser on your forehead.)

Line: *"Don't ask."*
(NO. This is a surefire conversation stopper—because they won't.)

Line: *"Hanging in, and you?"*
(YES. Nothing wrong with boring. It's better than

morose. But you better hope the other person has
something to say.)

Line: *"I'll be much better after I have a drink!"*
(YES. I like this one. But you have to be sure of your
crowd.)

Line: *"Oh my god, just wait till you hear about the terrible
things that have been happening to me!"*
(NO. "Wait till I hear?" Hmmm. Why don't I just wait
over on the other side of the room and talk to some
other people.)

Line: *"To tell the truth I'm only so-so this evening. Actually
I am more interested in how you are."*
(YES. An excellent response, providing it does not
come off as fake or condescending.)

Line: *(With a grateful, warm smile) "Until now, I have to
say I was having quite a bad day."*
(YES. This is the very best line, and can double as a
romantic line. You never know, with a line like this,
your whole miserable life could turn around, fast.)

THE SECRET OF LISTENING

The best way to turn your bad mood around is to get out of
your own head and into the head of someone else at the party.
It's true that, for various reasons, some people are better listen-

ers than others are. You might be someone who needs to listen better. It's nothing to be ashamed of. Truly good listeners are rare, and it is definitely a skill you can hone.

Understanding the Problem

So why are some people "bad listeners"? Contrary to popular belief, minglers who have trouble with listening are not always egotists or narcissists. There are a lot of other reasons for this issue.

Fear: Much of the time it is our own feeling of vulnerability that causes us to lose focus. We are afraid of not reacting to the conversation correctly. We may realize that we don't know a reference that's been made and are concerned that we are going to appear stupid. Just as your physical muscles tense up when you are afraid, your brain tenses the same way. It's very common to blank out a little when you are nervous and/or self-conscious. You could be worried about your bra strap showing, or whether you have lettuce in your teeth. You could be afraid you are going to be caught not remembering the person's name. Mostly, you could be worried that you won't have anything to say when it is "your turn" to speak. Steven Inskeep once posed a question to me when I was being interviewed by him about mingling for NPR's *Morning Edition.* He quoted a line from the movie *Pulp Fiction,* "Do you listen, or are you just waiting to talk?" I don't think he meant me personally, but it made me think. One of the things that happens to us sometimes is that we have something we really want to say and worry we will not remember it. In those instances we just have to let it go and hope it will come back to us later. And if, when it does come back, it is no longer appropriate to the conversation, we simply have to move on. Because it is more important that we be engrossed in what is being said than it is that we wow someone with a clever remark.

Hubris: Sometimes I think the reason people lose interest, or drift off, is because the mind thinks it is capable of doing more than just listen to the spoken words. Especially if what the other person is saying is not too complicated or deep, there is a part of the listener that might think: *I can listen perfectly well to this and also plan out my menu for tomorrow, without anyone else suspecting, as long as I just keep smiling and reacting.* So a competing thread starts in the listener's head, because he is under the illusion that he has brain power to spare, that he can mentally multitask. He believes he's being efficient. But the notion that we can actually listen to someone with one part of our brain and do something else with the other is a fallacy; both functions suffer. This tendency has been made worse by the sound-bite life we all live now: texting while walking, doing homework while watching a video, surfing the web or emailing while talking on the phone. We actually feel great pressure to do more than one thing at a time. When someone calls me on the phone, I immediately get up and do the dishes or make the bed while I'm talking—so I won't "waste" time. As the tasks I am doing are mindless ones, I never think it affects my conversation, when actually it does. Those times I do just sit in an armchair and concentrate fully, I have better conversations.

Distraction: Even those of us who don't have ADD have days when what has been happening to us makes it harder to pay attention. You could be feeling pressure that you should be talking to an important client who you noticed just walked into the party. You could be worried that your boyfriend seems to be spending an awful lot of time talking to a beautiful blonde. It's also hard to listen to small talk if you are in the middle of a personal crisis, or you are waiting to hear from your child who was supposed to have texted you two hours ago. In these cases it is sometimes best to let the other person know you are distracted and why, so that he will understand if you are having trouble listening the way you know you should.

Hearing Aides

Mostly, people who are less than great listeners just have bad habits that are not that hard to change with a little effort. Here are some ways to practice good listening skills.

Listening Between the Lines: When describing the techniques in this book, I occasionally talk about surreptitiously scanning the room in order to know where to move next or to avoid trouble spots. However, if you are someone who often has trouble listening, you should practice doing nothing else but focusing on where you are—just *be* in the conversation you are in. A good way to get in the habit of engaging the entire part of your listening brain, rather than simultaneously using part of your brain for something else, is to try to hear what the person is *not* saying, as well as what they are saying. You have to listen not only to the words coming out of his mouth but also to what is behind the words. Try to decipher other facial and body signals. What does the other person smile at, when do they seem most animated? Latch on to what is pleasing her; uncover her motivation for choice of topic. Pretend you are a private detective, or a brilliant therapist. Who is this person? Is she happy? Is she nervous? Prompt her with thoughtful questions that will show her that not only have you been listening, you have practically read her mind!

A Farwell to Hmmms: We all know that making empathetic noises is a good thing to do when you want to let others know you are paying attention, but we also know that "Hmm," and "Uh-huh" is what people usually say when they have turned the listening machine in their heads to autopilot. It's very easy to get lulled into the lazy rhythm of responding this way. So make an effort to use other more colorful or specific encouraging words, like "I always wondered about that," "I didn't know that," "That's totally amazing," or "Your boss must have been impressed." These reactions will require that you truly listen, which of course is part of the idea of this practice.

Wait, Don't Jump: Resist the temptation to finish other people's sentences. Interrupting with "Me too!" may seem like an act of bonding, or empathy, but it's not. It's only frustrating to the speaker when he can't complete his story. So try not to jump in too quickly with "That reminds me of the time I . . ." or "That happened to me!" Of course, it's okay to swap stories, but you must make sure the other person has finished his first. Let the person have his moment, his story. A good conversation is a genuine, organic back-and-forth, like a game of catch. In essence, the person speaking needs to toss the ball back to you before you start talking. And if someone else in the group interrupts, wait until that second person is finished, and then turn to the original speaker and say, "So, you were saying that you . . ."

Think of it this way: Instead of making your point, help them make their point. Being a generous conversational partner will endear you to others.

Of course, sometimes your listening capabilities are just fine; there is nothing at all wrong with your attention apparatus. It's just that what you are trying to listen to is some blowhard pontificating about a political cause or an obsessed video gamer bragging endlessly about his "sick" performance on level 30 of League of Legends. If this is the case, it may be time to bail out and move on.

4

The Great Escape: Bailing Out and Moving On

When I speak of escaping, I do not mean leaving the social event itself. I'm talking about something much more difficult: how to remove yourself, as gracefully as possible, from a conversation. As almost everyone knows, getting into a conversation may be hard, but getting out is often much harder.

A friend of mine told me a story that reminded me just how necessary escape sometimes is. He attended a party—a business function—even though he had recently hurt his back and was in a fair amount of pain. Although he had gone to the affair with hopes of forgetting his troubles, his physical discomfort caused him to bring up the subject of his injury with a fellow guest. "You hurt your back?" the man said with unexpected animation. "Boy, are you in for it now! You're going to have trouble with that now for the rest of your life! Let me tell you . . ."

Realizing his mistake in introducing this literally painful

topic, my friend tried weakly to change the subject, even going so far as to say that he really wasn't in the mood to talk about it. But the guy would not stop.

"Believe me, I understand. What are you, about thirty-five? I hate to say it, man, but it's all downhill from there. Listen, half my friends have chronic back pain. But, whatever you do, don't have the surgery. You'll never be the same again, I'm telling you . . . What you really need to do is . . ." Helplessly, my friend tried to edge away, but the man had found his prey; he went right along with him. It was a most unpleasant experience and went on for what seemed an eternity. My friend swore off parties for two months after that.

I have heard hundreds of similar stories over the years, though most of them are not quite so terrible. Most of the time it is simply a question of being stuck in a conversation with someone when you would like the opportunity to talk to other guests present. The key to having a good time at parties is being able to choose whom you talk to, and for how long.

Personally, I find that extricating myself from a person or small group takes more effort than entering even the toughest of groups. In fact, it can be so difficult to get away from some people that many minglers just give up and settle in, resigned to the fact that they are probably going to be with this person for most of the evening. It often seems easier to stay put than to make the effort to move, especially if the current conversation isn't too dreadful. I even know one man who actually tries to get stuck; he seeks out another person at the party who shares his desire to stay in one place, with one person, the whole night, so that he won't have to worry about entering or exiting conversations.

Don't take the easy way out. The term "mingling" implies talking to more than just one or two people; if you remain in one place with no clue (or inclination) as to how to move on, you're not mingling, no matter how great a conversation you are having. Naturally, if you discover the love of your life or the most fascinating person in the universe (or both, if you're lucky!), you may decide to stop moving around and stay where you are. That's okay, of course, but it isn't mingling. Mingling means circulating. And to circulate successfully, you have to know *when* to make your move, and *how*.

WHEN TO MOVE

Boredom and Other Discomforts

The most obvious reason to move on is your own misery. Everyone has a personal tale of excruciating agony, that time they were hopelessly stuck with Mr. Highly Obnoxious or Ms. Painfully Boring. Usually a kind of inner panic sets in, and you try to talk yourself through it ("Okay, I'm going to get out of this . . . Oh my god, this is terrible . . . Why doesn't he just shut up for one second . . . Okay, I know I can get out of this some-how . . ."), while on the outside, you smile with a glassy stare (the aforementioned Glaze-Out) and act as if you are listening. There's never any question about it in these cases. You need to get out as quickly, as gracefully, and as permanently as you can, whether you are imprisoned by a ditz, a drunk, a monologist, a wolf, a bigot, or just someone who has a disgusting amount of hummus stuck in his teeth. Remember, you can be selfish at a party. No guilt feelings are necessary; you are there to have a good time. *You* decide not only what to drink and what to eat, but also who to talk to—and for how long.

Wrong Fit

Have you ever gone into a bar and, while you are still standing in the doorway, immediately got the feeling this was not the joint for you? In mingling, once in a while you may realize you are simply in the wrong group, as if you've landed your spaceship on the wrong planet. Let's face it: The party only lasts so long, and there are a lot of people to meet. You don't want to spend too much time in conversations that are uncomfortable or unrewarding. Here are some signs you may not be with compatible conversational partners and you might want to move on ASAP:

Some of the people are using offensive language or are vehemently touting ideology opposite to your own.

There exists an air of meanness or rudeness (vitriolic gossip about the hostess, for example).

There seems to be a conversational "cult leader"—that is, it's obvious within a couple of minutes that one person is monopolizing the conversation; everyone else is standing around in a state of stupefied admiration like groupies. (This is fine if the leader is someone you would like to listen to.)

You experience Alien Being syndrome. This doesn't happen often, but once in a while you are with people who just don't seem to get you, and you don't really get them either. You're not connecting on any level, no matter what you try.

Saving Face

The great thing about large parties is that if you happen to make a faux pas, tell a joke that no one else thinks is funny, or otherwise embarrass or humiliate yourself, you can leave the witnesses behind and start with a clean slate somewhere else. Just forget your failure and try again with someone new.

The Case of the Vanishing Group

This phenomenon can be frightening to the minglephobic. Usually it begins without your even being aware of it; suddenly you notice there are fewer people in the group in which you have been engaged. The smaller the group gets, the harder it is going to be for you to get out. Also, in the case of the vanishing group, there is usually a reason for its sudden shrinkage; namely, there's one person in the group who is an irritant in some way. (Let's hope it's not you.) If you don't watch out, you're going to be the last one left, trapped with him or her, like the last rat on a sinking ship. Keep your eye out for the vanishing group, and leave before it's too late!

Time's Up!

Optimum mingling time is five to fifteen minutes per person or group (though there are some conversations that last three minutes and some—if they are really great—that may last thirty or more). You may be having a wonderful time, but you must move on. I know it's hard to leave when you're having fun, but remember, you are there to talk to as many people as you can. Tell yourself that you can come back to this person after you've met seven more people. Or get the person's info and ask him or her if you can get together one-on-one at another time. Take the good energy generated from the successful interaction and inject it into your next encounter!

Warning: Overzealous minglers may, on the other hand, move too quickly. I must plead guilty to doing this sometimes. I get so into the motion of mingling, the excitement of interaction, that I sometimes realize I am spending only sixty seconds in one place. And that is definitely not enough time to do anything but leave a "Who was that masked man?" feeling behind.

THE ETIQUETTE OF ESCAPE

Knowing Where You're Headed

Before employing any of the escape techniques described in this chapter, it's essential that you have a clear idea where you are going next. Ideally, your next target will be a person or group, but you can also set your sights on a place (the bathroom, the bar, the food table, etc.). Many of the following escape lines include a mention of where you are headed, and of course you must at least pretend to do whatever you announce you are going off to do. If you decide you just want to walk around, be sure to plan your general route or direction in advance. For one thing, if there is any time other people may be watching you (which, as I pointed out in Chapter 1, isn't likely), it's when you are leaving and entering cliques of people. Movement catches the eye, and if you break away from the group and are uncertain where to go next, you could end up looking lost and unwanted. The longer you are alone, not attached to any group, the more alienated you can feel, until you end up wondering why you left your last conversation anyway and how you can get back in. More important, if you don't appear to have a definite destination, the people you've just left could feel insulted, realizing that you would rather be alone than talk to them.

Always remember, the best time to scope out the room is when *you* are talking, especially if you are with only one or two other people. When someone is talking to *you*, you are required to maintain eye contact. If you are in a larger group, however, you may be able to scan unnoticed when the attention isn't focused on you. But please try never to be caught looking off across the room, making it obvious you wish you were somewhere else!

The Five Laws of Survival

Mingling has its very own set of rules, some of which are different from the traditional standards of etiquette. Since it is during escape maneuvers that your sense of courtesy and graciousness will come in direct conflict with your instinct for survival, here are five rules to govern your exit behavior as a mingler, rules that you will find especially helpful to remember as you get ready to break away.

1. **It's okay to tell a lie.** That's right. As I've said before, forget all that stuff you learned in school about George Washington and the cherry tree. George was probably terrible at parties. Lying for the purpose of mingling well is most assuredly in the "white lie" category (see The Philosophy of Fibbing, page 24), and it's absolutely essential for most exit techniques.

2. **No one knows what you are really thinking.** Even the best psychics can't read your exact thoughts. For the most part, other people know only what you tell them and what you show them.

3. **The other person is thinking primarily about himself.** This is not just a mingling rule but a life rule. It helps to remember this one if you are nervous about someone seeing through you, or if you are overly worried about what someone else thinks about you.

4. **It's better to escape from someone than have someone escape from you.** This law is a good motivator if you tend to procrastinate too much while preparing to escape; there's nothing more awkward at a party than being left standing by yourself.

5. **Change equals movement; movement equals change.** This is the most profound law and applies to all aspects of mingling (as well as all aspects of life). The only real crime in mingling is stasis.

THE GETAWAY: TWELVE EXIT MANEUVERS

The Buffet Bye-Bye and Other Handy Excuses

Without question, this is the most commonly used escape technique, especially among men (there are, in fact, some extremely fascinating gender differences in mingling). What you do here is wait for any sort of lull in the conversation, then deliver any of the following excuses:

"Excuse me, I've got to get some food."

"I'm going to get something to drink."

"I must powder my nose! (Yes, I sometimes use this vintage euphemism, just for fun.) Macho man version: *"Pardon me, must find the john/hit the head."* Cutesy cat-lover's version: *"I have to visit the sandbox."*

"Excuse me, I have got to locate my husband [wife/boyfriend/fiancé/ roommate]."

"Pardon me, but I simply must sit down."

"I have to go outside to feed the meter/for a breath of fresh air/for a cigarette."

"Do you have the time? . . . You're kidding. I'm so sorry, I have to make a phone call."

In spite of the ease with which these familiar excuses can roll off your tongue and their popularity among most partygoers, I myself do not use the Buffet Bye-Bye more than is absolutely necessary. When you use the BBB, you must actually *do* what it is you have just announced you will do, even if you don't feel like it, and even if you are fairly sure your escape victim isn't looking. This can really cut into your party fun. Plus, you can end up overeating, or drinking too much, or—worse still—*standing in line for the bathroom when you don't need to go!*

The other, very real danger with this technique is that the person from whom you are trying to escape may offer to go with you to the food table, the bar, the couch, outside for a smoke, or even to the bathroom. (The only really safe excuse is the telephone line.) There is nothing for you to do in that case but agree cheerfully and hope you can shake them off at the specified location, using another method. Also, depending on the situation and how old-fashioned you are, you may feel it's rude not to offer to get the other person, or even the whole group, a drink, if you use thirst as your excuse. While it is, in general, acceptable to say you'll "be back" and fail to return, *never, under any circumstances,* is it permissible to promise someone to fetch them a drink and then not return, though I know people who will deliver the proffered drink quickly and then move on. But it's not always easy to do this smoothly.

Celling Out

In spite of the universal trend to incorporate smartphones into every aspect of our waking reality, I believe they must be used sparingly at a party. When you are trying to meet and bond with new people, phones should basically stay in your pocket or your purse. Used in moderation, however, cell phones do provide an excellent ruse for extricating yourself from hard-to-leave fellow guests. The conceit must be that your phone is on vibrate, as it is almost never good manners to have your phone on ring at a party (unless you are outside, or the party is very loud and crowded—or you have a sick family member at home). Try to wait until a lull in the conversation, say "Oops" or "Shoot!" and go for your phone. Glance at it (the key to successful cell phone subterfuge is the look on your face; you must look aggravated at the interruption), shake your head apologetically, and move away from the group to a quiet corner or room to deal with your "important message" (that is, to return the email/text). Afterward you can rejoin the party—in another group of course, as if you were pulled there inextricably or you just forgot where you had been before the interruption.

Your cell-phoniness can double as an exit from the party itself, should you find that you are desperate to leave before it is particularly polite to do so. If you do decide to leave the party, you can fabricate any number of believable, even intriguing, stories about who contacted you and why you have to leave. Or you can just be cryptic: Wave your phone in the air dramatically and say, "I'm sorry, I'll explain later, but I must leave right away," and dash out in a flurry.

Smartphone watches can make Celling Out even more facile; with one glance down and a light tap on your wrist, you can excuse yourself for any number of reasons. However, the very ease of this ploy may negate its efficacy, as probably everyone will be doing it all the time. I have to say, as Miss Mingle, I welcome the advent of smartphones attached to people's wrists about as much as farmers welcome an early frost.

The Honest Approach in Reverse

When I talk about "honesty" in mingling, I'm not usually talking about truthfulness (which has nothing much to do with mingling) so much as a kind of *straightforwardness*. If you're like me and tend to be direct, you may want to use this exit technique whenever possible. It works only if you have been with one person or the same set of people for a respectable amount of time (ten minutes or so). As sincerely as possible, say something like, "Well, as enjoyable as this is, I think it's time for me to go mingle," or "Well, I don't want to monopolize your time, and anyway I think we're supposed to mingle at this thing." Or you can use a version of one of the opening lines (page 39): "Excuse me, but I really must go practice my mingling!" This maneuver constitutes a strong, definite form of exit; it announces your intention to leave in a manner that is not open to negotiation, and at the same time it offers an excuse that is more honest than many of the excuses people usually use to escape. It is, in fact, the most truthful line you can employ without admitting straight out that you find the prospect of continued conversation with them unappealing.

Note: This exit technique works even better when it is coupled with the Honest Approach entrance. If your opening line has already established you as an guileless person and an enthusiastic mingler, people are going to buy this exit line much more readily.

The Fade-Out

This one needs very little explanation; it is something that almost everyone who has ever attended a large party has done. It is appropriate for those times when you're not too involved in conversation—and hence you are not really trapped—and you simply want to move away as unobtrusively as possible.

As you may guess, the directions for the Fade-Out are the exact opposite of those for the Fade-In technique (see page 28).

Wait until no one is talking to you or looking at you too closely, and then . . . slowly start to back away. Watch and listen carefully as you begin your disappearing act, in case the conversation should happen to turn back to you in mid-fade. When you feel you are far enough away from the group to be unnoticed, make tracks!

Two warnings: You must not try this unless you are in a cluster of four (counting yourself) or more. Otherwise, you can be caught during Fade-Out, and that can be extremely awkward. If you are caught—and this may happen, even while leaving a large group—you need to switch immediately into another escape tactic. So have one ready, just in case.

The Changing of the Guard

This well-known exit maneuver was one I had actually forgotten about until one night I attended a cocktail party on Manhattan's Upper East Side. I had set my mingling sights on an attractive man I had met very briefly earlier in the evening. He was standing in a group with two other people. I used the Fade-In (with just a smidge of the Touchy-Feely Mingle, something I'll talk about later), addressing my first remark to the man who was my primary target. The second I was "in," the other two guests took off, but fast! I was stunned by the sudden realization that my entrance had given them a way out and that this passive escape technique is used all the time, by practically everyone. I was so floored that my mouth fell open, and I just stood there like an idiot, staring at the disappearing duo. (I was soon reminded of another truism, vis-à-vis the attractive man: Looks can be deceiving.)

This exit method works because of law number five: *Change equals movement; movement equals change.* As soon as a new person, or a new energy, enters the circle, a readjustment of some kind, no matter how subtle, automatically occurs. It's as though the new person has kicked up psychic dust, and while everyone is waiting for the dust to settle, people can slip away. I also call this strategy the Substitution Illusion, because the person exiting is using the illusion that because a new person is taking his place, it is now okay for him (the exiter) to leave. It's a fascinating aspect of mingling, and makes for a totally facile escape. The drawback is obvious: To use the Changing of the Guard, you have to wait until someone new arrives. And it could be a very long wait.

The Smooth Escape

When you can pull this off, it makes you feel great—like a champion of minglers. It does, however, require a bit of fancy footwork. What the Smooth Escape has going for it is that it works in drastic situations and, when done well, it's so subtle and natural that no one realizes they've just been handled.

The three steps of the Smooth Escape are: (1) Take control of the conversation. (2) Change the subject. (3) Exit. Easier said than done, I know. But here's an example.

Say you started out talking to a circle of four or five people but, one by one, they have peeled off until you are left alone with Showy Joey, who has you pinned in a corner and is talking nonstop about his job as an office furniture salesman. Having failed to detect the Case of the Vanishing Group in time, you are now in one of the most challenging spots for any mingler.

Don't despair. You *can* get out of this. But take a deep breath and concentrate, because you are going to need to be more alert for the Smooth Escape than you have been (as evidenced by your current predicament) so far.

The first thing you must do is focus totally on what Joey is saying, so that you will be able to seize the slightest opportunity to wrest control of the dialogue. For example, as he is saying "so my real problem has been that in this economic climate, most people are demanding a discount even on our most rock-bottom clearance price, and still they expect all the bells and whistles . . ." you can break in with, "By 'bells and whistles' do you mean things like potted plants or do you mean things like those fancy conference room phones?" *(You've taken control.)*

"Why . . . sort of . . . I mean the conference phones are only . . ." Joey might continue. Interrupt him again with something like, "I always wondered who pays for what. When I see these huge fica plants in offices I always assume the building is responsible for them, and I also always wonder how these plants have enough light for them to grow. Or are they fake, but just so real-looking you can't tell? You know, I used to really hate all artificial plants, as a general rule, but now I'm on the fence about it." *(You've changed the subject.)* While Joey is busy trying to switch gears to follow you, keep talking. "The thing is, artificial plants don't use any water, or take any labor for their maintenance, so that means a low carbon footprint . . ." At this point, while you are still speaking, focus on something across the room, as if something irresistible has caught your attention, touch Showy Joey's arm lightly and say, "Excuse me a moment, won't you?" (And smile. It's always a good idea to be as warm as possible when you're leaving someone high and dry.) Then move quickly away. *(You've exited.)*

The Smooth Escape can be a bit tricky, but keep the following in mind: If you act as if the conversation has been brought to its natural close, and that you've had a lovely time talking to Showy Joey but the dance is over now, your behavior won't come off as rude. Don't forget, Joey has probably been run out on at parties most of his life. To him, it may feel normal. The important thing to remember is that when you are really stuck with someone, the only way to get away is to take control of the situation.

Shake and Break

This escape route also involves taking control, but you have to have just the right circumstances to execute it properly. Use it only at a very large party, preferably a business party, when you are sure you are not going to mingle again with the same person or cluster. In other words, you have to be making your way through a large room of people, intending to leave when you have covered everyone; or you have to have a *very* good memory and avoid your Shake-and-Break victims for the rest of the night.

Suppose you are up against a super talker like Showy Joey. As you are smiling at him and responding facially to what he is saying, stick your hand out until he instinctively takes hold of it, or just grab his hand (this won't work if he's got his hands in his pockets). Shake it until he either stops speaking or at least slows down; then smile warmly and tell him "It's been so nice meeting [talking with] you!" Then turn and walk away. In the opposite situation, where you are trapped with Mr. Awkward

Silence, the Shake-and-Break technique is even easier, as you will not have to interrupt the flow of conversation. Just shake . . . and break!

The Human Sacrifice

Most people are too ashamed to admit that they use this device to escape from undesirable mingling partners, but I see it done at almost every gathering I attend. It's a clever maneuver because it poses as a social grace. The only prerequisite is that you know at least one other person at the party.

Imagine you are engaged in what seems an interminable discourse with a woman who is telling you about her new vegan cookbook . . . recipe by recipe. Before your mind numbs out completely, look around you and locate someone you either know or have just met. Proximity is important; you are going to have to be able to reach out and shanghai this third person. While nodding enthusiastically to what the vegan is saying, pull this new person into your little twosome. Immediately you will feel a shift, a loosening of the woman's hold on you. Introduce the sacrificial lamb to the vegan in a way that implies you are just being a good mingler by introducing two people who will probably have a lot in common. *As soon as their eyes meet,* leave immediately. You must fade out of the conversation within thirty seconds or this conversational change of partners will not work. A pleasant "Excuse me" will also serve as an alternative to a Fade-Out. As in ballroom dancing, you can't be considered rude since you have procured a new partner before moving on. But do remember the key here: *As soon as you have finished introducing the new person,* either do a fast fade or leave in a more overt manner, but get out quickly.

This trick works for the same reason the Changing of the Guard works: You've changed the cast of characters; you've brought in your own replacement. Of course, the more sophisticated minglers will know exactly what you're doing. In fact, I've been used as a sacrifice many times; I can spot the maneuver almost as soon as I'm summoned, but there's not much I can do except to find another sacrifice as soon as I can or escape in some other manner. Obvious or not, the Human Sacrifice is still a perfectly acceptable move. All's fair in love and mingling!

Please keep in mind, however, that if you wait passively for a Human Sacrifice candidate to pass by, you could be stuck with the vegan till the end of time, or the end of the party, whichever comes first. It's easiest if someone does pass right by you, of course, but there are many more active versions of this ploy. You can take the vegan (if you're alone with her) by the arm and, while conversing, gently lead her across the room to another person or group. If she won't budge, you can interrupt her and say, "Do you mind if we join my friend over there?" Or even "Hey, this is making me hungry, let's go get some food [a drink]!" Once over by the food, where there will be a large cluster of people, you can lure a stranger into the conversation and then skedaddle, even if you have to use the bartender.

The Personal Manager

If you can't find a Human Sacrifice, you can try to motivate the person to leave *you*. This tactic requires a little acting skill and a lot of charm. Point out someone else in the room and say "Oh look, there she is! . . . That woman over there is dying to meet you." Or, "I'm sworn to secrecy but there's someone in that group there who is giving out free theater tickets [gift certificates/expensive cosmetics]." (Be sure to be vague about who this supposed philanthropist is.) Or wave in the general direction of a group and say, "I think you're being summoned." When your victim looks confused and asks, "By whom?" tell him, "I can't see him now, but he was waving to you . . . over there." There are countless ways of seducing the person into leaving you (you can tell him the food is disappearing fast or that there's only one bottle of champagne left), and the great thing is, you can keep inventing until something works!

Escape by Mutual Consent

In all likelihood, this won't happen very often. When it does, it will result in great relief and maybe a slight amount of embarrassment.

Sometimes two people who end up talking to each other will realize at more or less the same moment that they are in a bad marriage, mingling wise—or that they are simply ready to move on. They will look at each other and be able to tell that they both feel exactly the same way; the dialogue between them is either played out, or they were mismatched in the first place. Usually one of them will smile sheepishly and say, "Well . . ." and the other will respond, "Well, it's been nice to . . ." and then the first one will say "Good talking to you!" And with a respectful nod or even a handshake, they'll turn away from each other at the same time and head off happily toward their next encounter. It's rare that such a clean and easy "divorce" occurs, but it does happen.

The Counterfeit Search

Try this technique at your next party and I bet you will have enormous success with it. It requires a little body language, specifically use of the eyes.

It's especially easy to flow into this exit ploy if you have grown weary of the person who is talking to you. Your attention is probably already drifting, and you are going to be using any time you can to look around the room—either because you are thinking about your next conversational target or simply because your interest is waning. Try to follow the rule about scanning the room only while you are speaking; however, this is one time it may be necessary to let your eyes rove a bit while the other person is speaking to you. If you remember to look at him intermittently you can get away with it. The trick is to give the impression that something inescapable is beginning to pull your attention away from your current conversational clique—totally against your will. To complete the maneuver, suddenly focus your eyes on someone (real or imagined) across the room and exclaim, "Oh!" Look embarrassed and confused for a moment, as if you didn't really mean to speak this out loud. Then smile apologetically and say something like, "I'm so sorry, please don't think me rude, but there's a person over there I've been looking for since I arrived; he is supposed to have some information for me," or "Excuse me, will you, I just spotted someone I haven't seen for five years!" Or, at a business function, "Pardon me, but I just noticed a person across the room my boss particularly instructed me to talk to."

The Counterfeit Search can be a little abrupt, but if you put enough energy into making it look sincere, it's one of the quickest ways to exit. It is indubitably a bold maneuver, which is the very reason it works so well. People don't suspect this kind of pretense; whereas, every time anyone excuses himself or herself for a drink or something to eat, it smells of escape. The other advantage to this technique is its quality of positive energy; you will appear to have so many people you need to talk to that you can't remain in one place—you're just dashing madly here and there! It can lend you an air of popularity. You may, of course, alter the line to make it comfortable for you. Some people prefer "What the . . . ?!" (as in "What the heck is *she* doing here!") to the above "Oh!" Use whatever comes most easily to you. Always leave your Counterfeit Search escape victims with the impression that you are going to come back to them as soon as you possibly can. So what if you never get around to it?

The Preemptive Strike: Dodge Ball

Sometimes your advance warning system can allow you to escape before the fact. In certain rare emergencies, you might need to execute this preemptive escape technique:

You are having a quiet moment alone, sipping your martini and surveying the mingling field. Suddenly you notice a new arrival to the party. It's a woman you absolutely abhor. Every time you see her she insists on gossiping viciously about other people who are present. To your dismay, she makes eye contact with you and you just know she is heading your way.

You've got to be quick on your feet to succeed at Dodge Ball. As soon as you see this woman glance at you, you must not hesitate—not even for a microsecond. Don't smile at her;

in fact, try to act as if you haven't seen her. Then make a bee-line for a cluster of people who know you and who will let you into their protective custody, posthaste.

Of course the woman may very well suspect what you are up to, which is why Dodge Ball should be used only when faced with the most torturous bores, barbarians, and bad guys.

EMERGENCY ESCAPE HATCHES

If you really want to improve your mingling skills, I strongly suggest you learn and practice at least a few of the twelve escape maneuvers I have described. However, for use in a pinch, here are some quick-and-easy (some would say down-and-dirty) emergency escape lines.

"Hold that thought . . ."

"I'll be back . . ."

"I'm sorry—I just remembered something . . ."

"Got to go mingle!"

"Excuse me just a minute, won't you?"

"I'm not feeling well . . ."

"I'm starving, excuse me . . ."

"Excuse me, it's my contact lens . . ."

"Uh . . . I think I just lost a filling . . ."

"Oh my GOD—my wallet! It's gone!"

5

Fancy Footwork: Advanced Mingling Techniques

Once you have some basic maneuvers down, you may want to try to expand your mingling repertoire and begin to fine-tune your mingling style. Remember, the more versatile and practiced you become as a mingler, the more enjoyment you will get from your social encounters, and the easier it will be to achieve whatever secondary goals you might have (getting a job, getting a promotion, getting lucky, or just getting through another office holiday party). And, though most readers may not immediately be able to master every one of the following techniques and tricks, I think you'll find many of them familiar, and some of them invaluable.

MINGLING STYLES FOR THE WELL-SCHOOLED

The Quick-Change Artist

The more you come to understand the art of mingling, the more you will see the importance of being in control of your conversations. A true mingling artist virtually shapes each encounter using various tools of his trade, the most powerful one being the ability to change subjects easily. Most natural-born minglers have this Quick-Change talent without even realizing it, and unless they are mingling purely by entertaining, the Quick Change is probably their forte—the skill that makes them indestructible mingling machines.

To become a proficient Quick-Change Artist, you need to practice shifting your focus a bit during conversation, so that as you listen to the other person speak, you concentrate not only on your response to the person's comment or question, but also on where you want the conversation to go next. I don't mean that you should not pay attention to the present conversation. The best minglers always at least *appear* to be fascinated by whatever is being said to them. But if you are on your toes, you can be ready to make a swift transition to a subject of your choosing before the people around you even know what hit them.

A good way to think about the process involved in the Quick Change is to imagine building a bridge. You and your conversational partners are currently on one side of the river; you want the group to be on the other side. The key is to find some material with which to build a bridge from one side to the other. If you simply interrupt and change the subject without making a connection between the old topic and the new one, you will usually come off sounding awkward or narcissistic. Remember, it can't look as if you have consciously manipulated the direction of the conversation; the dialogue must appear to flow naturally, as if it is taking its own course.

Let's say your conversational group is composed of a very interesting architect, the architect's husband, and another person. You would like to steer the conversation around to the architect, as you have seen her buildings and admired them. At present, however, the architect's husband is going on at length about his garden, which you personally find about as interesting as cardboard. Everyone else is standing there, passively listening, or making innocuous comments such as "Oh I've seen those, they're beautiful," or "Do those bloom all year round?" As a Quick-Change Artist, you can decide exactly where you want to be, conversationally, and it should take you no time at all to get there. Imagine all the possible connections between the two subjects, select one, and then head for the bridge.

For instance, you can turn to the architect and say something like, "Planning houses in a community is like planting a garden in a way, isn't it?" Or, "Do you work closely with the landscapers on the gardens and lawns for your buildings?" The architect will answer, and you will be able to continue in your chosen course of conversation, taking pride in the fact that you have succeeded in creating a more interesting environment not only for yourself, but also (probably) for at least two of the other three people in your clique.

Admittedly, some subjects are harder to move away from than others. And there are some people who are adamantly determined to talk about whatever it is they are determined to talk about. If you really get good at changing subjects, however, you can outmaneuver anyone and/or escape if necessary.

Another way to approach the Quick Change is to use free association. This method can really keep the ball in your court, which is where you want it, because it's always an advantage if *you* get to serve. For example, if someone is chattering away about flowers, take the word "flower" and let it lead you to another word, the first word that pops into your mind. In other words, think "flower—bee." Then ask, as if it is really puzzling you, whether or not bees pollinate all flowers, or just some. When the flower aficionado answers, you can then safely complete the subject switch by remarking that you have an uncommon fear of bees, or that you are allergic to bees, or did everyone know that after bees sting you they die, and isn't that true justice? This last remark can lead to a discussion of aggression and justice, which can end up being a whole lot more interesting than flowers and fertilizer.

Free association is used often by the Quick-Change Artist for two reasons. First, it's more flexible and open-ended than bridge-building. That is, you aren't necessarily trying to get from point A to point B; you are simply moving away from point A, either because A is boring or distasteful to you or because you want to be in control of the dialogue. Second, free association works well for this technique because the subject you move to is probably right on the tip of everyone else's brain, also. The change will usually seem perfectly natural and not at all forced. A good Quick-Change Artist can, in this manner, lead the conversation of a whole group rapidly and elegantly from one topic to another, so that everyone, including the Artist himself, has a good time.

The Pole Vaulter

A more extreme form of subject changing is called Pole Vaulting. A Pole Vaulter is someone who is a facile topic jumper and a master of the non sequitur. People who can completely change subjects in the blink of an eye—without coming off as either demented or terribly ill-mannered—command amazing power in all their interactions. If you can Pole Vault well, you can actually leap right over to where you want to be.

Given the garden conversation example above, a fairly pedestrian Pole Vault subject change might be something like: "There are so many different kinds of flowers . . . I can never tell one from the other; I'm handicapped that way! . . . But hey, before I forget to ask, how old do you think this apartment building is?" Or, "Well, I don't know about that, but I do know that I'm starving at the moment." In both cases there is a short kind of wrap-up before the actual Vault. More abrupt, without the wrap-up, would be a sudden interjection like, "Have you heard that Donald Trump is getting another divorce?" which even if it isn't true is intriguing enough to lead someone off the track.

Some subject changes are more imperative than others. If you sense someone is about to bring up the touchy subject of your soon-to-be ex-wife—in front of your girlfriend—you might interrupt/derail him with an alarming non sequitur like "Excuse me, but is that a mole? On your cheek there? You better get that checked out, that doesn't look too good." Other generic non sequiturs include "I'm sorry, I just this second remembered a strange dream I had last night," or even "Wait . . . I'm having déjà vu!"

Warning: Do not use the Pole Vault when you haven't been

listening. (This technique is not intended as a substitute for the Dot-Dot-Dot Plot.) It is important that no one is in the middle of a conversation about the death of their dog or their upcoming cancer surgery when you start vaulting. You could end up landing flat on your face.

The Playful Plagiarist

Have you ever been in a wedding reception line where you had to talk to hundreds of people, one right after the next? You probably had absolutely no idea what to say to any of them, and your face started to hurt from trying to smile so much. It was while in such a desperate situation that I—happily—stumbled upon the Playful Plagiarist style of mingling. It's perfect for reception lines, award ceremonies, and other occasions where you are the center of attention (your coming-out party, your art opening, your fiftieth birthday) and people are coming at you, fast and furious.

Let's say you are the maid of honor at a wedding. As if it weren't bad enough that you have to stand there in a horrible peach chiffon maid-of-honor getup, you are being forced to stand in your dyed-to-match, uncomfortable pumps and shake hands with an unending stream of guests, most of whom you don't know and couldn't care less if you ever saw again. You have only a couple of minutes to speak with each person, and because all you really want is for reception-line duty to be over so you can have a drink or something to eat, your natural tendency is to take a totally passive stance—that is, to smile as nicely as possible and say "thank you" to the obligatory comment that you certainly do look beautiful and the ceremony was so lovely.

This is, of course, perfectly acceptable social behavior. But if you consider the fact that the guests moving through the line are just as bored as you are at having to take part in this outmoded reception-line ritual, why not try to make it fun? Having fun is, after all, your objective in every mingling situation. And believe me, if you can make interesting conversation in a wedding reception line, you can do it anywhere. Here's what you do.

Take something someone says to you, and use it on the next person who approaches you, as if it is your own idea. For example, if Mrs. Smithers says to you in parting how nice it is that the bride and groom found each other after all these years, when Mr. Johnson greets you next, you can ask him if *he* doesn't think it's wonderful that the bride and groom have found each other after all these years. Then when Mr. Johnson says, yes, they make a lovely couple, you can say to the next person, don't Joe and Sally make a lovely couple? And when that person says Oh yes, she's never seen such a beautiful bride, the next thing on your lips can be a remark about how the bride is the loveliest bride you've ever seen.

By using the Playful Plagiarist, you can avoid using one line over and over, and at the same time you don't have to think up new things to say at sixty miles an hour. Although the examples I have given might not be too hard to think up yourself, in tiring mingling situations it's much more relaxing if you let others do some of the work. A little conversational petty theft, and people will get the impression you have a natural social sense. In fact, it will appear as if you are never at a loss for words.

The Playful Plagiarist technique can be useful in "normal" party circumstances also, though it may call for a little more panache in its execution. At a typical large party, using this style requires taking a line or comment you hear in one group with you and delivering it when you are safely inside another group (sometimes you can even use it as an entrance line). For example, if someone remarks that this is the tenth party your host has had in one year, the next time you are in another group of people and in need of something to say, you can repeat the line, especially as it is a general party observation and will fit in at just about any pause.

Warning: Occasionally, someone may recognize your stolen line as having come from someone other than you, either because there's a witness from the first group present or because the comment has unmistakable characteristics. If you think there's any possibility of getting caught with your hand in the till, the best thing to do is give authorship: Start or follow the line with "So-and-so was saying that . . ." That way no one will think of you as an unoriginal sap who is reduced to stealing bits of conversation—yet you still get to use the material!

Trivial Pursuits

Some people have a gift for remembering bits of trivia, others (like me) don't. There's no way that I know of to change a non-trivia-minded person into one of those human fact magnets we all know and love. However, if you *are* an automatic storer of trivia, you have a great asset to your mingling style, as long as you keep in mind the following:

1. **If you've got it, flaunt it.** If you do have interesting tidbits of information at your fingertips, by all means share them.

Trivia and mingling are close cousins—they're both light, interesting, nonthreatening human interaction. But keep it within reason, please. No one enjoys talking to someone who spews trivia every time he opens his mouth.

2. **Wait for an appropriate place in the discussion.** This is absolutely essential in playing the mingling game of Trivial Pursuits. Your fun fact must be relevant to the conversation and be offered up in just the right place, so it doesn't seem forced, or as if you are showing off your trivia prowess. For example, if you suddenly want to bring up the fact that the word for having a fear of getting peanut butter stuck to the roof of your mouth is arachibutyrophobia, there'd better be some peanut butter being consumed at the party.

3. **Don't maneuver the conversation for the sole purpose of delivering a piece of trivia.** This is taboo, even though good minglers have the skill to do it. If the item you have is so earth-shatteringly fascinating that you feel compelled to offer it, just jump in and do it, if you must. But don't spend time and energy manipulating the discussion so that your piece of trivia will fit in. You may get caught at it, and that can be *very* embarrassing. In fact, to put it bluntly, you could end up looking like a Trivia Nerd. Trivia buffs are considered entertaining only if they are not too obsessed with their trivia.

4. **Make sure of your audience.** Watch carefully when you deliver your first trivial fact. Do the others in the group seem interested? Sometimes people find certain trivia to be

an intrusion in the flow of dialogue, or even boring. There's no way to tell whether or not you use trivia well except to study the reactions of those around you. Do eyes roll or glance away? Do you hear a lot of throat clearing? Make sure you're not being obnoxious.

The Art of Piggybacking

Piggybacking is a very familiar concept in mingling, and I know many people who rely on it as a mingling style. It's not exactly the most courageous tack to take, but it can be used continually, from your first opening line up until the time you leave the party.

Many minglers use this technique without thinking about it, it's so simple. It entails merely attaching yourself briefly to another person to get from one place to another.

Imagine that you arrive at a party where just about the only person you know is the hostess. No problem. Just latch on to that hostess and hang on for dear life (figuratively speaking, that is—you are *not* encouraged to actually hold on to coattails or skirts during this maneuver) until such time as she leads you over to someone else and introduces you, or until someone new joins you and the hostess. Have no fear, for one of these two things will happen within minutes, if she's any kind of hostess at all. Now you have a new acquaintance to tag along with, and you can follow this person into another group, where you can find new people to trail. In this way you can leapfrog from conversation to conversation, always appearing to have many friends and never being at a loss for a conversational companion. Even if, for some reason, the hostess *doesn't* hook you up with another guest but just gestures to the far end of the room and says, "Feel free to help yourself at the bar," you can still employ the Piggyback technique—after you've introduced yourself to one or two people using other methods first.

The real art of Piggybacking lies in the way you follow people. Like a good gumshoe tailing someone, pretend you don't notice when your Piggybacking target leaves the circle of people; wait a few seconds, and then casually follow in his wake. Remember the Changing of the Guard escape technique? It's very easy to move off right after someone else has exited, if you do it quickly enough. The idea is to make your target think, when he sees you've followed him into a new group, that it's only a coincidence, or that you found his conversation interesting enough to want more of it.

Please note: It's essential that you remember to switch piggyback targets as often as possible. It's against the basic precepts of mingling to stay with one person for any substantial length of time. Never forget my earlier maxim: *He who mingles best mingles alone.* (Of course, I never said you couldn't occasionally have a little help.)

The Butterfly Flit
(experts only)

Picture a country meadow on a summer day. In fact, if you can, go visit a country meadow on a summer day. Watch how the butterfly dances lightly upon the flowers. Notice how quickly and gently she touches each one, barely brushing like a whisper over some while resting gracefully for long moments on others. The butterfly flies free; each flower she visits is honored by her brief stay, and each perfumed encounter becomes forever a part of her fluttering experience.

Pardon me for waxing poetic, but this is the image you must hold in your mind while attempting the challenging Butterfly Flit. It is with this technique that mingling becomes an art form, and like any true art, it is hard to describe in concrete terms or by using step-by-step directions.

The Butterfly Flit can encompass any or all of the techniques, lines, and tricks in this book. Using all the mingling knowledge and instinct at your disposal, your objective is to weave your way through the clusters of people, stopping for thirty seconds or so at each to check them out. If you decide a group is interesting or challenging enough for you to make a mingling commitment, you enter the group more fully, and remain for a five- or six-minute period. Then you're off again, leaving your ex-group breathless, wishing you had stayed longer and hoping you'll return soon.

Just exactly how, choreographically, you manage the Butterfly Flit without being impolite to anyone or knocking anything over is too complicated to describe. If you are ever feeling truly inspired or socially brilliant, go ahead and give the Flit a whirl. It's one of those things you can learn only by doing. But, frankly, I do not recommend it for most minglers.

GIMMICKS FOR THE CONFIDENT MINGLER

When the circumstances are right and you are feeling game, the following gimmicks can add spice to your evening and variety to your mingling experience. Unlike the styles described above, however, mingling gimmicks are for occasional use only. Your limit per party should be one or two times for each trick.

A Case of Mistaken Identity

I know you've probably seen countless versions of this ploy in bad "B" movies. Historically it has been used as a pickup line, which is why I try never to use it except when my motives are purely conversational. You guessed it; it's the old "Pardon me, I thought you were someone else!" This is such a cliché that it actually works, probably because most people can't believe anyone would try this line if it weren't true.

There are many enjoyable and effective ways to carry off this daring opening maneuver. The easiest and safest is to come up behind your "mark" and confidently touch or tap them on the shoulder. Your big "I'm so glad to see you" smile should fade by the time the person finishes turning around, and be replaced by a confused, sheepish, surprised look. Then you can say something like, "I'm so sorry . . . from the back, I swear, you look just like someone else [my old roommate/my neighbor]." I sometimes even like to add, "God that sounds like a line, doesn't it?" Anyhow, by this time you've more or less entered the group and you can go ahead and follow your Mistaken Identity entrée with any number of conversational moves, including just plain introducing yourself.

There are, as you can imagine, more outrageous ways to use a Case of Mistaken Identity, all of which can make a lasting impression but can also get you into trouble. You can pinch the person, slap him smartly on the back, even kiss him on the neck. All of these things imply an intimacy that must be equaled by your embarrassment when you discover your "mistake." The drawback with these more extreme versions: Often the victim is so confused and the other people in the group so startled, that the thought of actually joining them becomes distasteful to you.

Always remember, however, that should this gimmick back-fire and you find yourself greeted with hostility, the very nature of the lie will allow you to withdraw without losing face. After all, it wasn't the person you were looking for, right? You didn't mean to approach this group anyway; it was all a mis-take. With a parting apology, you're out of the group, free and clear, ready to try it again (on someone on the other side of the room, please) or to put away the gimmick for another day.

The Interruption Eruption
(experts only)

Please pay attention to the Experts Only label on this one. Even I rarely attempt this stunt, though it's a heck of a lot of fun when it succeeds. You have to be feeling absolutely fearless.

Let's assume you *are* an expert mingler, with years of expe-rience under your belt. You are at a fun party and are feeling adventuresome. You have just ducked smoothly out of a conver-sation you had grown weary of and are scanning the room for a new set of mingling partners. Suddenly, you spot it: a laugh-ing, glittering cluster of four or five people over by the cake. They look like a tight group, an invigorating challenge for you to try to enter. You quickly run through the many entrance ma-neuvers in your mind and decide on . . . the Interruption Erup-tion. When you feel ready, you take a deep breath, move boldly up to the group, push your way firmly in between two people—

without waiting for them to stop talking—and say, loudly and with great energy, "Hello there! How are you all? Hey, I don't think I've met a single one of you yet! My name is . . ."

It's not so much what you say in the Interruption Eruption as how you say it. Your demeanor must communicate that you know that everyone will be happy that you've come to talk to them, even though you have more or less exploded, uninvited, into their conversation. As you may suspect, there is a danger- ously thin line between this technique and being obnoxious; so the important thing is to exude extreme warmth to everyone in the group after you are in. You must positively *beam* good- will at everyone, and at the same time you must lead the con- versation for a few minutes. People will expect you to perform after such an entrance.

You can use almost any line for the Interruption Eruption; you can even use a question, such as one of the Game-Playing questions on page 55 ("Excuse me! What color would you say this is?"). A question is usually a bit more abrasive here, but if it is a very good question, one that someone will snap up right away, it can be a quicker way in. The best kind of question to use is one that indicates an ongoing debate or poll taking, such as, "Hey, what have you guys heard about the Smith company warehouse burning down?" Not only will your eagerness for information help excuse your interruption but also people tend to forget that you've barged in on them when there's an interesting query before them.

The Interruption Eruption is a strong, daring mingling gim- mick, which can be positively thrilling when you are victori- ous. However, if it doesn't work, you are in serious, serious trouble. One time I interrupted a group with a brazen, "Hi,

guys! Gosh, isn't it hot in here?" Well, you might have thought
I'd just hit someone. Everyone looked at me with a mixture of
distaste and astonishment, and one man said, "Excuse me . . .
we were in the middle of a conversation." Upon which I slunk
away, tail between my legs. But of course I recovered. And so
will you.

The Quotation Device

Many of my acquaintances swear by the Quotation Device.
For some sticky situations—and especially in certain circles—
this particular gimmick can be just the thing to create a sense
of camaraderie among strangers. If you have any sense of the
dramatic at all, you will discover that if you aren't using this
one already, you should be.

Here's how it works: When someone says something that
makes you or anyone else feel uncomfortable, or when you are
at a loss for something to say, or just if it seems like the perfect
moment, just pop in one of the following famous quotes from
movies or television shows. Your listeners will love it; it relaxes
most people immediately. Whether we like to admit it or not,
television and film are more of a common denominator than
race, religion, financial status, or occupation. Especially these
days, since we are currently enjoying a new golden age of television. People are always referring to their favorite shows.

What you are actually doing with the Quotation Device
is relieving psychological tension by calling forth a common
cultural image. Sometimes, you recognize the line but don't
know where it came from. It still works because it's part of the
cultural lexicon. It almost always lightens the atmosphere, and
it has the added benefit of being the kind of conversational

punctuation mark that can allow you to change the subject or even exit from the group. Two rules: The line must be familiar to people (different references work in different crowds—for example, if you are at an event with a theater crowd, a Chekov quote might be just the thing), and you must quote it correctly.

Note: You are *not* to cite the source of the quote unless prompted. (Anyway it's usually a bad sign if they have to ask!)

Here are some of my favorites. (Please note: I lean toward the classics. You will come up with your own references.)

LINE	USE
"I think this is the beginning of a beautiful friendship." *(Casablanca)*	When flattered, for general amity, or right before you hand her your business card
"Frankly, my dear, I don't give a damn!" *(Gone with the Wind)*	When insulted, or when dealing with unwanted news or gossip
"Years from now, when you talk of this—and you will—be kind." *(Tea and Sympathy)*	After a faux pas, like right after you have asked a nonpregnant woman when she is due
"Leave the gun, take the cannoli." *(The Godfather)*	When you are behind someone at the bar or buffet who has been lingering for a long time, making it hard for other people to get by
"I'm afraid I can't do that, Dave." *(2001 Space Odyssey)*	When someone asks you to do something you don't want to do at a party (such as, play beer pong, sneak onto the roof, etc.)

LINE	USE
"Fasten your seat belts. It's going to be a bumpy night." (*All About Eve*)	After having witnessed an argument or an insult, or upon seeing the host's uninvited ex-wife arrive
"That's a horse of a different color." (*The Wizard of Oz*)	When stalling for time, or trying to diffuse an argument
"Help me, Obi-wan Kenobi!" (*Star Wars*)	When you've made an embarrassing faux pas like forgetting the name of the host
"It is a far, far better thing I do than I have ever done." (*A Tale of Two Cities*)	Upon setting off to get someone a drink, after having been asked to do any favor, or when heading toward a long bathroom line
"No soup for you!" (*Seinfeld*)	At the buffet table, upon realizing the food is gone, or to heal awkwardness after some kind of food faux pas
"Is that your final answer?" (*Who Wants to Be a Millionaire*)	When someone answers a question and you think he is totally wrong
"Shall we go for the 'Full Monty'?" (*The Full Monty*)	When going for seconds at the buffet table
"Beam me up, Scotty." (*Star Trek*)	When you've just knocked over a lamp or revealed to Bob's girlfriend that you used to date Bob
"We're going to need a bigger boat." (*Jaws*)	Upon a shift in the party atmosphere—the arrival of a large group, or when someone brings out a case of tequila

Party Favors: The Helpless Guest Gambit

Brace yourself, because this is probably going to be distasteful to some people. All I can say is that I've seen this method employed all my life, by both children and adults, and it works. It's kind of a knock-down, drag-out way of mingling, but I must confess that even I have used it on occasion, with spectacular success. If done well, the Helpless Guest Gambit can make you the star of the party.

Ready? Think of yourself as a damsel in distress (or a knight in need—this is a gender-equal ploy) and the other guests as your rescuers. If you put people in the role of helping you, it: (1) gives them a purpose, (2) flatters them, (3) leaves you in control, and (4) most important, gives you something to say.

My favorite version of this technique is getting someone to "protect me" from someone else. For example, after my opening, I'll say something like, "Listen. There's someone here I'm desperately trying to avoid. I can't tell you who it is, but you'd be doing me a big favor if, when you see me doing this"—and I show them some subtle hand or eye signal—"you'd just come over and check up on me if you can." Naturally, people want to know who it is and why I am avoiding them. I won't be able to tell them, of course, having made the whole thing up (I can claim I am protecting the other's identity), but it makes for great conversation. Also, usually what happens is that the person or people will keep checking up on me to see if I need protection even if I don't give the signal (which I usually don't). If you tell a few different sets of people this story, you can get a big rush all evening, and everyone will wonder what your secret power is.

Another, often more subtle, way to play the Helpless Guest is to ask as many people as you can to help you obtain information.

You can say to person X that you heard an important business contact was going to be present, and would X mind letting you know when the contact arrives. If X doesn't know the contact, you can still ask X to keep her ears open for anyone who does. You can mention to person Y that later on in the evening you will need a ride home, and if Y should happen to meet anyone who he knows is going in your direction, to please let you know. When introduced to person Z, you can ask him for yet a different piece of information or use one of the ones you used before.

It doesn't matter what information you request. The important part of this gambit is that when X, Y, or Z says he doesn't have the answer to your question, you say, "Well, do me a favor and let me know if you do find out." That way, if you query enough people, some of them will return throughout the evening to report to you. Getting people involved with you in this manner is your insurance against being a wallflower and can really liven up your mingling experience.

Making the Most of Toasts

Most people make toasts only at weddings or awards dinners. Toast making at a sit-down dinner is a pretty straightforward proposition, but contrary to what you may think, a toast can be made anywhere, at any time—even while mingling.

"Anytime" is a slight exaggeration. You do have to have a glass in your hand to make a toast. But given that small requirement, you can throw one in at practically any juncture, for various effects. For instance, you can recover from a faux pas ("A toast! To carpet cleaners!"), soothe an argument ("Here's to a difference of opinion"), field an insult ("To charm—something you might like to learn more about sometime!"), or even exit from a group ("To [whatever is being discussed] everywhere! Excuse me.").

You can throw in a toast in the more obvious situations, of course, such as after someone has just brought you a drink ("Here's looking at you—thanks!") or after somebody makes an announcement ("To Jeff's new job!"). You can also use toasts to change the subject—specifically to take the heat off yourself, if someone is asking you questions you'd rather not answer or is making you uncomfortable with too much attention. Simply pick out someone else in your group and make a toast to him, or take the too-personal subject and make a toast to the subject in general.

Usually you will want to wait for a pause before proposing your toast. But often, if you simply raise your glass while someone is still talking, the speaker will pause—sometimes in midsentence—and you can make your toast. All of us are trained to stop whatever it is we are doing and pay close attention when someone raises a glass. Toasts are very powerful social weapons and can be an important part of your conversational arsenal.

Two toast tips: (1) Never down the entire contents of your glass after a toast, unless you have only a small amount left, or unless you are in a place (Russia, for example) where this might be considered the norm. (2) If your glass is empty when someone proposes a toast, just raise the empty glass in tribute. *Don't* pretend to drink, and *don't* say, "Hold that toast until I get something in my glass" (unless it is a party-wide toast; in that case there will be a designated glass-filler nearby).

SOPHISTICATED BODY BUSINESS

Not all conversing is done with the mouth. Your whole body speaks every time you move. Body language is important to learn for all areas of life, but for the would-be mingling expert, there are three particular pieces of body "business" you may want to study.

The Mysterious Mingle

The Mysterious Mingle is really about poise. So far in this book I have been telling you what you can say, when you should say it, and how you should say it. But there are times in mingling when the best line to use is no line at all.

To carry off this technique, you must project the attitude that you have a great many fascinating things to say, but that *tonight* you'd rather listen to others and kind of soak up life. Some Mysterious Minglers prefer to put a little ho-hum feeling into their presentation; others lean more toward the intriguing "I've got a secret" look. In either case, your posture must be erect but nonchalant, and your facial expression should be attentive, pleasant, and, above all, confident. It may help you to employ the Celebrity Magic survival fantasy (page 14), at least for the first time you try this.

As you move through the room, keep your arms and legs relaxed, and don't hurry anywhere. The world is your oyster. Life is a bowl of cherries (and any other platitude of this nature you can think of). You are going to listen contentedly to conversation, and answer thoughtfully when called upon, but never with more than a few words. Use an enigmatic smile whenever you can (practice this—it has to *look* enigmatic, not just feel it). Whether you are quietly entering a group (this is the only time you're allowed to use the Fade-In without completing the maneuver by saying something), exiting a group, or just standing by yourself somewhere, remember: You are not at a loss for words, you've just put them away . . . for now. By choice. Your body stance, your eyes, mouth, eyebrows—every part of you—has got to say, "I like people very much but I really don't care at all what they think of me."

There's something very powerful about a person who does not talk when everyone else is working so hard at conversation. If you do the Mysterious Mingle well, people will be so interested in trying to find out what your story is and why you're not talking about it, that you could find yourself becoming—silently—the center of attention.

Note: It's not a good idea to try to get away with a Mysterious Mingle pose when you suddenly find you can't think of anything to say. People will sense the difference, unless you are an extremely good actor. There are, after all, other, much easier things to do when you draw a blank. Also, be sure you are coming off as mysterious and not supercilious. You don't want people to think you just can't be bothered talking to the likes of them.

The Touchy-Feely Mingle

Never underestimate the power of human touch. A small amount of the right kind of touching while you are mingling can add a comforting sense of warm intimacy to your conversations. The wrong kind of touching, however, or too much touching, can be one of the most serious faux pas you can make without falling on top of the dessert.

When employing the Touchy-Feely Mingle, always err on the side of not enough rather than too much. Even when you are flirting with someone at a bar, where it's possible you may initiate a little more physical contact than you would if you were mingling at a business function, be conservative. If you have to, tell yourself you have only so many touches to give out for the whole night so you have to use them sparingly. And—though this may sound sexist—men need to be much more careful with the Touchy-Feely than women do.

Use the Touchy-Feely when you are involved in a fairly absorbing conversation with one other person. It doesn't have to be a tête-à-tête—there can be others standing with you in the group—but you and this other person should be doing most of the talking. Watch the other person's face carefully to see if he or she is truly engaged in the discussion. At an appropriate place during a time when *you* are speaking (the punch line of a joke, the climax of a story, the main point in a discussion, or when you are getting ready to end the conversation) lean forward slightly and clasp or touch the person's forearm or upper arm briefly, then let go. It should not be *quite* a squeeze, yet more than just a brush. Now, and this is important, regard the person carefully during this touch, watching in particular the eyes. You should be able to tell if your touch has enhanced the exchange or hindered it. Unless you are certain that the effect was a positive one, *do not touch this person again.*

Other types of Touchy-Feely mingling include resting your hand briefly on the shoulder of someone standing next to you, touching someone lightly on the back (not the small of the back, please, that's a little *too* intimate for mingling), and taking someone's elbow as you move across the room together. For the most part, any other kind of touching during mingling is unacceptable. The Touchy-Feely Mingle, when done with sensitivity, can make a five-minute conversation a warmer, more enjoyable experience. But remember, a little goes a long way. There's nothing quite so unpleasant as being repeatedly pawed by some ham-fisted lout.

Fumbling-In

This one is really an entrance maneuver. Some people might find it crude, but advanced mingling doesn't mean subtlety; it only means that the methods require more skill or finesse. So while Fumbling-In may seem like a rough-and-tumble way of entering a conversation, it actually takes an accomplished mingler to perform it correctly.

This is the exact opposite of the Mysterious Mingle. The perfect model for this gimmick is Clark Kent. His character, who seems on the surface to be a naive klutz, is really a superhero who can disarm people with his clumsy act. It is with Clark Kent's particular form of graceless artfulness (or artful gracelessness) that you are going to approach this opening gambit.

Select your target group. Edge toward them, making certain no member of the group is looking at you. With your back or at least your side to them, pretend to be concentrating hard on something across the room, and then . . . "accidentally" bump into someone in the group. But not too hard; for this particular trick, you don't want to cause drink spillage or personal injury. Just jostle them enough for at least one person to notice and acknowledge your presence. After you say you're *so* sorry (this has to be convincing) it is usually easy to join their conversation. If, on the other hand, you should be confronted with any hostility, like "Look where you're going, why don't you!" have some believable explanation ready. "Pardon me, someone pushed me" is always good, though I also like the more self-denigrating "I am *so* sorry, really, I don't know what is the matter with me—I've been a clumsy oaf all day!" With the latter excuse you still have a chance that your fumble will succeed; your taking responsibility for your klutziness may endear you to some of the group and alleviate some of their initial bad humor.

The real beauty of Fumbling-In is that, if the gimmick does fail and you are ignored or rebuffed, or if you decide that you made a bad selection and you don't want to stay in the group after all, it's the easiest thing in the world for you to move on. You can't be rejected, because you didn't ask to join their group; it was an accident! In effect, nothing has been ventured, and therefore nothing is lost.

Note: Fumbling-In should be attempted only in a fairly crowded room. If there are miles of space between people, you're just going to look foolish; or worse, drunk. It's bad enough if you do get drunk at a party, but it's an absolute crime to *appear* drunk.

The Swivel

Another of my favorites for a crowded room is something I call the Swivel. It's a little like a dance move, and it can serve as an exit and an entrance maneuver combined. You have to be standing within a group of three or four people (not counting you), and those people must be engaged in an animated conversation with each other. Here are the steps for the Swivel:

Step one: While smiling and remaining aware of your group's conversation, stop contributing and begin to listen to the conversation that is happening directly behind you. If it is a crowded party this will not be too difficult, unless the music is really loud. (If the music is truly deafening, your choice of mingling techniques will be limited to the most primitive ones. I myself have never understood the desire for super-loud music, unless it's a dance party.)

Step two: When you have heard enough of the rear conversation to be ready to contribute with a quip or a question (à la the Fade-In from Chapter 2) just turn your head around a bit, sort of suddenly, as if someone has just called your name or said something so relevant to you that you were pulled toward them inexorably. It should look almost against your will, almost as though one of them had tapped you on the shoulder.

Step three: . . . and—swivel! I sometimes imagine pivoting in field hockey when I do this. As soon as you have turned 180 degrees, move slightly away from your old group, who hopefully are so engrossed in the conversation they will hardly be aware of your twirl. Then complete the maneuver by offering the new group your quip or question.

The swivel can make a crowded party more fun and can shake you out of a party stupor if you are falling into one. Obviously, you must not swivel when someone is talking to you. As in the Fade-Out (Chapter 4), you have to conversationally disengage first.

CONVERSATION PIECES: USING PROPS

Jewelry and Accessories

Whether it's a cool feather hat or a pin that says "Clone me," wearing an unusual accessory almost guarantees that you'll never have to endure the trauma of the Awkward Silence. Invariably, the first (or second) thing people will say to you is "Wow, what a wonderful (odd, awful, unique, colorful) ___ that is!" Not only does your prop provide them with easy subject matter—for which any minglephobic is always grateful—but it also causes them to introduce a topic for which you're totally prepared. You are now on home turf, because it's your accessory, after all, and you have probably already had many conversations about it. You have stored up a wealth of material from which to choose (where you got that particular hat, about wearing hats in general, the origin of hat wearing, etc.), and you've already rehearsed your lines.

Before it became practically a felony, I was a dedicated cigarette smoker. I also had *the* coolest, most extraordinary, most beautiful cigarette case anyone has ever seen, which I bought at a flea market in Paris. It was made of sleek, blue-and-white Art Deco plastic and contained fourteen separate cylindrical compartments that held one cigarette each. It had springs, so that when you bent it in two you would expose only one cigarette. Whenever I took out this case, people would ooh and ah and ask to examine it. It was a superb mingling prop. But I never knew just what a treasure I had until one fateful night in Chicago.

My friend Cathy and I had decided to check out a bar we had heard was "popular." We had never been to the neighborhood before, and when we got there, I knew why. The cab left us before we had a chance to turn back. "Oh well," we said to each other, "how bad could it be?" We certainly weren't going to be chicken.

P.S.: We should have been chicken. A big hairy guy with

rings in his nose let us in. A smirk on his face plainly said, *These little girls don't know what they've just gotten themselves into.* We looked around nervously. This was in the eighties, when punk bars were really punk—scary places with chains and knives and danger. Cathy and I didn't know much about punk bars. But we were about to find out.

Everyone stopped talking when we walked in. (I might mention that we were wearing fifties-style swing skirts and sweaters with sweet little pearl buttons.) All we could see were big tattoos with arms attached and dark, scabby faces staring intensely at us. Gulping, we stepped gingerly up to the bar and tried to act as though we were not in terrible trouble. The bartender, a huge man with a couple of safety pins through his cheek, leaned toward us and glared.

"Uh . . . um . . ." I managed to say, "Bombay martini, please?" Cathy smiled a brave smile. "And a Miller Lite?"

Silence. Nobody moved. Panic was closing in; I could feel Cathy tensing. Any minute we were going to have to get up and run, but run where?

I decided I really needed a cigarette. That's when it happened. As soon as the bartender spotted my cigarette case, he growled, "Lemme see that thing." Trembling, I handed it to him. He studied it, opened it, and then . . . he smiled.

In that split second, the entire bar relaxed. Our bartender, who turned out to be a rather decent fellow named Christopher, showed the case to everyone in the place, and we were immediately accepted. The cigarette case had, miraculously, been our ticket in. This mingling prop saved the day; in fact, we ended up having a surprisingly good time.

I'm not saying that your prop will keep you from being

killed as mine did for us, but there is no question that a prop can give you something to do as well as something to talk about. In fact, I don't think there is any single trick in mingling that works so well, so easily, and so often as having your own mingling prop of some kind. While purists might cast a scornful eye on the use of these obvious and common mingling crutches, I believe that anything that helps you have a good time at a party is legit.

The best conversation pieces by far are earrings, hats, and eyeglasses. (Unless it's a beach party, no sunglasses, please. No matter how cool they are, sunglasses hide your eyes, one of the most important connecting tools you have.) These props work best because they are worn on the head. The next best are pins, necklaces, scarves, and ties. Once you get below the waist—with shoes, stockings, pants—you are in more personal territory; things that are attached to the lower part of the body enter the area of personal attire. And most people will at least hesitate before commenting on your clothing—unless someone has on such an extraordinarily striking outfit that it would be almost rude *not* to comment.

Below is a list of accessories, in order of effectiveness, that can assist you in your mingling experience. Pick an accessory that is particularly beautiful, funny, cool, unusual, thought-provoking—or handmade by you. Note: If it's got a symbol on it, or words in a foreign language, be sure you know what it is you're saying!

earring(s)
hat
eyeglasses

tattoo

pin/brooch

handbag

necklace, watch, bracelet, ring

tie, scarf, shawl

a fan (Fans would be too theatrical in some circles, but
   on a hot summer day, why not?)

a baby or small child (A newborn baby, should you happen to have one with you at the party, is of course the
   perfect foil; however, the conversation will be mostly
   limited to the child, and when the crying starts, the
   conversation will stop.)

purse dog (Warning: Small dogs, while a huge draw, can
   be just as much trouble as babies.)

The Dumb Use of Smartphones

There is one "accessory" that in my opinion makes a very
poor mingling prop. In fact, it is a hindrance rather than a help.
Much has already been written on smartphone etiquette, and
because cell phones have been around for a while now, most
people these days have some sense of what crosses the line from
practical use into bad manners.

Or so I thought until last Christmas. I was attending a holiday cocktail party held in the lobby of a friend's apartment
building, held for all the residents. When I got there I was grat-
ified to discover that there was excellent champagne, gourmet
food, and elegant surroundings. I looked around, surveying the
mingling arena and . . . good grief! There, over by the food
table, was an extremely well-dressed man who with one hand
was dipping into the crudités and with the other was crudely

cradling his cell. He was actually talking on the phone while he was grazing the buffet!

This is one of the worse cases of bad phone etiquette I have witnessed firsthand. Perhaps this man was having some kind of emergency or was in the middle of a crucial business deal; however, it is also possible that, upon entering the party, he realized there was no one there he wanted to talk to, and reached for his cell. No matter what his story was, if I had been the etiquette police I would have arrested him on the spot.

Naturally, how and when we use cell phones in social situations is in part a generational thing. What would be considered "dumb" use at a party of twenty-year-olds may be much different at a party of sixty-year-olds. You can call me a stickler if you want, but when you are at a large party with people you don't know very well, here are the rules:

1. **Don't take or make calls and don't check your messages.** Unless you are employing the Celling Out escape technique (see page 85), you should keep your phone out of sight as if it were one of your private parts. Also turn the ringer off. (If possible, put the phone on airplane mode, as even the vibrating can be annoying at a quiet party.) If your wife is about to have a baby, you are allowed to check your phone. If you have a sick child at home or are a doctor on call you are allowed to check your phone. In almost every other situation, the best minglers will have their phones set to silent—better yet, turned off completely—and in their pockets. Before there were cell phones people were forced to

be wherever it was they were. Now the perception is that you will have a richer and more efficient social experience if you are connected in reality and in the virtual world simultaneously. The problem is every time you engage with your phone you are in essence leaving the party, causing a subtle but definite break in whatever growing connection is happening in real life. It's important to remind ourselves that multitasking is sometimes just a way of getting a lot of things done less well.

There is another thing to consider here, what I call the Eye for an iPhone syndrome. Invariably, when one person in the group gets out their phone to check messages, others will follow suit. They may have been successfully resisting the itch, but once one person has broken the rule, others figure, *If he's doing it, I can, too.* Plus what else is everyone supposed to do while they are standing around waiting for the person to check back into the conversation?

2. **Don't look things up**. This may the hardest rule to obey. Even I find it difficult. We have instant knowledge at our fingertips, immediate access to the answer to any question. And so the inevitable happens. Just when a conversation has begun to take on that wonderful organic spiral—with one subject leading naturally to another—accompanied, perhaps, with more and more laughter and a heightened feeling of connection, someone will invariably stop to look something up on his phone—either to confirm some factoid or simply because of the irresistible call of cyberspace (a drug few of us can resist for more than an hour or so). Of

course, the information is usually pertinent. But once someone breaks the flow by going "off-party," the social energy in the group tends to dissipate.

For instance, let's say someone is talking about a certain song. Before you know it, someone is looking up lyrics to that song, and then to another song, and then someone else is texting a friend to find out who sang the acoustic version, and then everyone has their phones out and begins checking their other texts and emails, and then they're on Twitter and Facebook. "Are you following me?" "What's your username?" "Have you seen this app?" Yes, you are still talking—it's an exchange of sorts—but you are no longer creating something between just the people present. The reason you came to the party is to mix with the people there; otherwise why come?

Anyway, believe it or not, sometimes when you can't remember the name of something, it leads to interesting discourse. It's a more natural way of creating the shape of the conversation. Plus, it's good exercise for your brain not to have Siri answer everything. Once a group of people start looking things up, it spreads like a virus, until soon what you have at the party is a bunch of individuals staring into their little blue screens, mumbling to themselves. A room full of partygoers with their eyes glued to their phones is indecorous at best, and the height of rudeness at worst.

It's more important to stay focused on the people right in front of us. So what if we don't know until we get home who was in that movie we all saw. So what if someone can't say for sure whether some article in the *Times* came out

Wednesday or Thursday. A party is supposed to be a sharing of fun, energy, and ideas, not an exchange of data.

I realize a lot of folks are going to disagree with me on this subject. It's unbelievably tempting to depend on your phone, it's the modern-day security blanket (or an extra brain) for adults and kids alike. It's also more addictive than cocaine and cigarettes combined. And I know if you are in your twenties having your phone in your hand is as normal as having shoes on your feet. Many claim having information at their fingertips actually enhances the conversation. All I can say is: Just humor me and try it both ways. The character of the conversation will change for the better without the phones, I promise. If you keep your eyes on the people in front of you, and use your own minds and memories for conversation, it results in a higher-quality human interaction. In fact I know a group of twenty-somethings whose very favorite thing to do together is to sit around the hookah. I am certainly not advocating smoking, but what I find interesting is that they say they never even touch their phones the whole time they are doing this. They just sit around talking for hours.

3. **No show-and-tell.** Please, don't show people you've just met pictures of your cats. Or kids, or dogs, or your family vacation. Unless someone asks for them specifically. Then you need to make it as brief as possible so you can get back to conversing. Note: "I love cats" is not a request to see your hilarious YouTube cat videos on the spot. You can always send them to the person later. In fact, it can be a great following-up tool (see Chapter 8).

4. **Paparazzi warning**. Recently a friend told me about a party he hosted where one of his guests happened to be a very handsome guy. Without warning, while Mr. Handsome was in the kitchen, another guest whipped his phone out and took a picture of him. Just like that. As if it were the most normal thing in the world to photograph someone you only just met while he's helping himself to pasta salad. Where did this photo end up? On Facebook? On Instagram? Twitter? Who knows? Because of the sharing possibilities, it is neither polite nor fair to take people's photos without their knowing about it. It's an invasion of privacy. Even if you are snapping friends, when you post those photos do not tag anyone unless you know the person is okay with it. Usually if the person you are photographing is under thirty-five they will think nothing of being tagged, but not always. Be sensitive to this issue. Some people enjoy posting their whole lives on Facebook, others don't.

Before you label me a total cybernazi, I must amend that if the gathering is at a bar or other public place (street fair, outdoor concert, tailgate party before a football game, rally, parade, etc.) most of the above smartphone rules do not apply. When you are mingling in public you are in a sort of "half-party" state. There are logistics to be handled, directions to be given, or photos of the band to take. It's understandable that you may need your GPS or access to your messages when you are out and about.

The Hors d'Oeuvres Maneuver

If you feel as though you need some kind of prop, but you've neglected to bring one with you, it may be the right time for the Hors d'Oeuvres Maneuver. This technique is a bit brazen, but it serves two purposes: It provides you with a piece of conversation, and it helps you move around the room freely.

You may be someone who has always had trouble circulating from one group to another and would like to try it with some mingling training wheels. First, offer your services to your host to pass a tray of food throughout the room. If the host gratefully accepts your offer, take the tray and just set off into the room. You won't have to worry about opening lines. Believe me, the minute people see you coming with those goodies, they will open a path for you. In fact, if the food you are carrying is appetizing enough, you can just stay in one place and end up with a crowd around you.

The best thing about this mingling method? It's automatic. Carrying a tray of food doesn't just *allow* you to mingle, it actually *forces* you to mingle, as it would be inconsiderate to the other guests to stay too long with one group of people.

Drawbacks: People may mistake you for the hired help. Also, you may find that the conversation, while you and your tray are present in the group, is limited to the food. In other words, people may associate you too much with the food, and not want to segue into other topics while you are standing there with your tray. Most important: If you are passing food, you can't be eating it at the same time. Eating off the tray you are passing is strictly prohibited. This can end up being too much torture to be worth it.

Working the Bar or Food Area

When asked what is the first thing they do upon arriving at a party, almost everyone I know has the same answer: They get something to eat or drink. I usually do the same thing myself. It's perfectly natural. But make sure you recognize the bar or food area not just as a place to sate your hunger or thirst but as a vibrant mingling center, complete with props and pitfalls.

I myself fell into one of those pitfalls at a Christmas party. The food table was laden with various delicacies; my undoing was some particularly exquisite smoked salmon placed at the head of the table. Smoked salmon is a passion of mine, and I'm ashamed to say I get quite greedy when I'm around it. I was doing a little mingling, but more or less hovering over the salmon, until I got an uneasy feeling I couldn't quite put my finger on. I mused over it as I took my tenth piece of salmon. Then it hit me. Instead of using the food area for mingling purposes, I had been using my mingling ability to get to the food! Specifically, to get to the salmon.

Never forget that your primary goal is mingling; food and drink should be a secondary part of your fun. They also can facilitate conversation. Here are a few simple rules for when you mingle in the food or bar area:

1. **Don't make a beeline for the food immediately upon your arrival.** Getting a drink right away is fine, but hold off for a little bit on the food if you can. People are less likely to introduce themselves to a person they don't know if that person is chewing. Once you have talked to a few people, you can go mingle by the food, and partake.

2. **Don't camp out by the bar or buffet.** Not only could you end up getting tipsy or sick (or both), it isn't considerate.

Some people won't have a chance to get near the bar or food if others won't move away. This rule is most important with respect to the bar. I know too many people who use their own minglephobia as an excuse to stand by the bar and guzzle drinks. Soon they find they have enough confidence to talk to anybody. But will anybody want to talk to them?

3. **Offer to help others get food or drink.** If you are standing next to each other, it's an excellent mingling ploy to help another person in some small way, even holding her drink for her while she cuts herself a piece of cheese. It endears you to the other person, shows you are a nice guy, and she more or less has to talk to you a little afterward, lest she be discourteous.

4. **Talk about the food and the presentation.** Party food makes for great, safe conversation. Talk about any unusual foods, ask another person if he knows what's in the dip, or to recommend something he may have tasted. Then let the subject of the food lead to other topics.

5. **Avoid making negative comments about any of the food unless the other person says something first.** You never know who is responsible for the cooking. Even if you are positive that no one at the party made any of the food, you could inadvertently insult someone; the dish could be exactly like one they make at home or brought to someone else's party last week.

6. **Try not to point with food or gesture with drinks.** It's unattractive and accidents can happen. And someone might get a breadstick in his ear.

7. **Make good use of the time you are in a line for food or drink.** Lines are great places for conversations (see page 158). They also happen to be the one place where it doesn't look funny if you aren't talking to anyone. If you're lucky, you'll have someone to talk to while waiting, but if not, you can use the time to scope out the party and map out a mingling campaign.

PLAYING DOUBLES: TEAM MINGLING

The best mingling prop you can have is another person. While it is definitely not advisable to stick like glue to your spouse or friend at a party, a partner can be a great asset if used properly. Regrettably, many partners fail to take advantage of this teaming-up opportunity—or even recognize the potential power they have as party allies. Over the years I have listened to countless complaints about partners at parties: husbands who mysteriously disappear only to be discovered off in a bedroom reading a book; friends who attach themselves to the people who brought them, never leaving them alone for a second; business partners who won't pull their weight in working a room full of clients; or wives who stand in a corner, too shy to mingle with anyone. More commonly, there is the couple who goes to a party and stands there talking only to each other.

The basic premise of team mingling is *not* to mingle as a

pair. You already see each other enough, and you won't meet as many people if you hang out together. Moreover, you will have a much better time, I promise you, if you venture off on your own. Split up, even if you come back to each other now and then to recharge.

However, mingling separately doesn't mean you shouldn't help each other. Teammates back each other up. And because you know each other well, there are numerous ways you can enhance each other's mingling adventure to double your power, double your fun.

Preparty Strategy Sessions

Preparty strategy sessions can be very constructive, especially for business partners. Before the event you might discuss what contacts may be present, and which one of you is going to schmooze whom. Also, you can decide which of you is better at what (Is one of you a great greeter? Is the other one better at entertaining people?), then encourage each other in what you each do best. In most couples one person is a better mixer than the other. This person is going to have to do more to help the less confident mingler. It is very much like playing doubles in tennis: If your backhand is weak, let her cover for you; if you're better at the net, then you need to adjust your stance accordingly. Determine how you can take the best advantage of your coupledom.

Conversational Procurement

This is a good technique for helping out a truly timid partner or friend. It may sound a bit complicated but will be well worth mastering if your partner suffers from minglephobia.

Basically, the idea is to lead as many people as you can, like sacrificial offerings, to your partner. Figuratively speaking, what you are going to do is to hand-feed her a virtual feast of conversations.

Step one: Let's say your wife has wallflower-itis. Upon entering the party scene, first guide your wife to someone you both know. (We'll call this hypothetical person Mack.) If you don't see anyone you know, introduce yourself and your wife to someone as soon as possible. Try to get your wife involved in the conversation right away using common conversational ploys, such as "My wife feels exactly the same way, don't you, honey?" "Mack, you must tell my wife about the time you . . . ," or "Get my wife to explain that; she's the only one I know who understands it!" Always be as complimentary to her as you can without embarrassing her, to help build up her confidence.

Step two: Excuse yourself for a brief period of time. Go get a drink or some food for the two of you, or put your coats in the other room. This will be your wife's trial separation. Make sure you return to her in five minutes or so with the promised drink or food. She must feel from the start that you are watching out for her, and that you will never leave her alone for very long.

Step three: If your wife and Mack are miraculously still chatting by the time you get back, give your wife an encouraging signal in the way of some kind of physical gesture (a slight squeeze of her shoulders, a hand on her waist) and say, "Excuse me, honey, excuse me, Mack, I've got to say hello to Georgie but I'll be right back." You then leave her with the accommodating Mack for the time being. If, on the other hand, Mack has escaped from your wife before you can return with the drinks, you then take her over to another person or group, get the conversation going as before, then leave her there.

Step four: From this point on, you will be bringing people over to your wife throughout the evening. For example, let's say you have been talking to a man for about ten minutes—perhaps he has been regaling you about the latest developments in genetic testing. Wait for him to take a breath, then say, "I'm sorry but my wife has *got* to hear this. She was just asking me about this the other night. I think she read the same article in the paper." Take him by the arm and physically lead him to your wife. Introduce them, and you're off again with a casual "Be right back." (This is technically not a lie as you *will* be back, again and again, delivering to your mate a constant stream of people with whom to converse.) Ideally, as the party goes on, you will have to feed your wife less and less, as she adapts to fending for herself.

Intraparty Playdates

You may have a partner who is so uninterested in mingling that it takes too much energy to assist him. Or maybe he didn't want to go to the party in the first place but you forced him to come. It's frustrating to try to help someone mingle who really doesn't want to . . . so don't. Instead, locate a similarly disposed antimingler and sit your non-mingling partner down with him. (When in doubt just pick someone who looks as if he may also be a party pooper.) The idea is to find someone *else* who seems repelled by the idea of mingling with a lot of people, someone who would therefore happily commit to a long sit-down conversation in a quiet nook somewhere. By matching your hermitlike husband up with a kindred spirit, you ensure that he is, at least in a small way, participating in the party. It may not be the perfect solution but it's certainly more appropriate than his being all alone in another room checking the game scores online.

Shepherding

If you happen to have a pathologically antisocial partner, one who resists even one-on-one interaction and will actually disappear into the host's study to sit himself down with a book, you may have to physically shoo him back into the mingling pool. Shepherding is a beefed-up version of what you probably already do—that is, to intermittently go find your partner and herd him back into the party. What will help you, however, is to enlist other shepherds to aid you so that you don't have to personally check up on him every ten minutes. Entreat one or two acquaintances to alternate with you in seeking out your lost sheep and firmly guiding him back to the main room under the guise of his being introduced to someone. Believe it or not, if the misanthrope is continually driven back to the party, he will eventually learn that his solitude is an impossibility. You may even find him returning to the party all on his own.

Reconnaissance and Rescue

Even the most confident people can (and usually do) use this form of team mingling, which consists mostly of an exchange of information. (It's like insider trading except that it isn't illegal.) It can be quite a handy thing to have an ally working the room with you; you can alert each other about mingling minefields and party pleasure points. With a word or two in his ear, you can help steer your partner to the most interesting people, as well as help him avoid the most uninteresting ones.

You can point out the deadly bore or the sloppy drunk so he won't have to go through the same unpleasantness you just did. Your partner can help you avoid the faux pas he has made; if he's just asked the host whether the young girl at his side was his daughter home from college, only to discover it is his new girlfriend, he can save you from making the same blunder. You and your partner can provide each other with names either of you may have forgotten. Throughout the party, you can check in with each other to see how it's going and to see if there is someone else present you need to give a little mingle to. Many couples even have signals they give each other when they want to be rescued from a person. (Try to be subtle—tapping the top of your head isn't recommended.) Usually a discreet movement of the eyes and raise of the brows will do it. Warning: Be very careful when whispering to each other about people at the party. It's a well-known component of Murphy's Law that whenever you say something really mean about someone, they are always standing right behind you.

The Mating Call

For this trick you don't even need the help of your partner, just the *fact* of him. This common escape technique is a couples version of the Counterfeit Search escape (see page 95). In this form of the Search, you make it obvious to the person or people you're itching to ditch that your mate is asking you to join him or her. If the ditchee knows who your spouse is, you can execute the Mating Call without using words; you can merely roll your eyes in the direction of your mate as if to say, *"He's calling me again!"* Or nod or wave in the direction of your mate, appearing to answer his or her call. If, on the other hand, the subject is not familiar with your mate, you can say, "Oh . . . pardon me, my wife wants me . . . excuse me for a moment, will you?" The "for a moment" is a nice touch and can soften the exit. It implies you really would like to come back to continue the conversation, but it isn't a promise. The brilliant thing about the Mating Call? It indicates you are leaving against your will, so it protects the ditchee's feelings. You just look loyal, at best; or henpecked, at worst.

Watching a good team at a party—two people who've been mingling together for many years—is like watching older couples on the dance floor. There is an in-sync, effortless quality about a good mingling duo. Mingling separately, they can seem more "together" than if they were circulating as a pair.

6

The Tailor-Made Mingle: Instructions for Specific Circumstances

Parties are like snowflakes—no two are alike. You can know all the entrance maneuvers, topic-finding devices, and escape techniques there are and still find yourself stymied, given a certain set of circumstances. Mingling at a Soho cocktail party is one thing; mingling at a Kentucky bluegrass festival is another. You need to know how to socialize with strangers in all kinds of situations, and be ready to navigate all different kinds of conversations.

NAVIGATING CURRENT EVENTS

Keeping up with the issues, trends, and news of the world is what makes us better citizens—and much better minglers. Of course, what people chat about at parties is different today than it was fifty years ago. For one thing, politics is now a dangerous curve lurking in the path of every topic. And in the wonderful new world of mingling, you have to be equally prepared to talk about nanorobotics as you are about nannies.

It's both easier and harder to keep up with today's news. We are bombarded with such an endless stream of stimulation and information that it's hard to process it all. Besides newspapers, we have hundreds of cable news channels and radio stations, and millions of news websites and blogs, as well as the distillation of the news on social media—an inundation of comments and video images. We are exposed constantly, even while waiting in line at the bank, riding an elevator, or—yikes—visiting a public restroom. Yet most of us know less about what's going on than we should, partly because of the "one story" or "viral" nature of the media universe, and partly because in our quantity-not-quality way of operating, we are more and more used to skating on the surface of things. Or perhaps the reason you don't know what's going on in the world is that you've spent all your leisure moments for the last four days streaming an entire season of *Breaking Bad*.

In any case, you don't want to find yourself standing at a party, a drink in your hand and a dumb look on your face, cut off from the flow because you aren't up on current events. Unlike many conversational experts, however, I do not advise you to tear desperately through a lot of newspapers and magazines right before the party. My feeling is that you're either tuned in to the world around you or you're not. No amount of last-minute cramming is going to make you a better-informed person. (Although it is not a bad idea to take five minutes to skim the headlines on a major news website like *The New York Times, The Wall Street Journal,* or *The Huffington Post.*)

You need to forgive yourself for not knowing everything. However, there are some situations in which you may feel truly mortified that you don't know what people are talking about— like a major scandal involving one of your own state senators, or a just-signed peace treaty between two countries who have been fighting for a long time—if only you could remember where!

Don't worry: There are some relatively simple strategies for dealing with those moments where you are suddenly and horrifyingly aware that you don't know what in God's name people are talking about (and you really should!).

The Zeitgeist Heist

Let's say you are standing in a group of people. Suddenly you realize the conversation has taken a turn and everyone is talking about a major mudslide. And not just any mudslide, but one that happened just two days ago and has been in all the papers and on all the news stations. It's a major event that you have somehow missed. People in the group are turning to you, expecting you to put your two cents in.

If you can't get away with maintaining a passive role, your best bet in this situation is something I call the Zeitgeist Heist. The first step in the Zeitgeist Heist is listening—not just to the facts but to the *feeling* behind the facts. You need to determine the issue or the theme of the conversation. Let's say in the case of the major mudslide that after a minute of listening to the discussion, you are able to ascertain that the theme of the conversation is not the tragedy itself but the fact that an increasing number of people are building houses where they shouldn't be allowed to build them. (Good: You've identified the conversational

Zeitgeist.) Then, at a suitable moment, you offer a remark regarding a residential area you know about in Delaware where they are building homes too close to the ocean, and so have to keep replenishing the sand dunes lest the houses get washed away. In all likelihood, the conversation will grow from there and your ignorance will never be spotlighted.

The Zeitgeist Heist differs from a traditional subject change technique because it is a way of joining in rather than distracting from—it's about keeping in sync with the *spirit* of the discussion. You are contributing, because your comment corresponds to the sensibility of the conversation. Is the issue the scandal of the thing? The tragedy? The politics of it? Are people more focused on how the media is reporting the story? It can be just as important to be in step with the essence of the discourse than to be up on the specific details of an event.

Please note: Make sure you have correctly comprehended the conversation before you jump in. I once had a fifteen-minute discussion with a friend about croquet—until I realized that *he* had been talking about cocaine! It was a rare case where the Zeitgeist was parallel. (He said rich people love to do it; I said it makes people mean; he said it's hard to find a place to do it . . . every comment we made was appropriate for each of the two very different subjects! Until finally he said, "I've seen a diagram of the molecule," and I knew something was wrong.)

Pleading Guilty

Of course, the other thing you can do (and what I often do) is to throw yourself on the mercy of the court. Covering up takes too much energy, and confessing your ignorance is the quickest way to become better informed on the subject at hand. After the initial embarrassment, you may be able to catch up to everyone. They may even admire your courage in admitting you don't know what's going on.

Say, "I didn't have a chance to read the paper or see the news today . . . where was the mudslide?" Or, "Oh! I think I heard a piece of that on the news today, but I didn't get any details." Or even, "Everything in the news stresses me out so much I confess I haven't been reading the paper at all and don't have any idea about that." (Note: Apathy being a national epidemic, this excuse is risky; some people may have little sympathy. And the embarrassment involved in admitting you can't remember the name of your own congressman may be too much to bear.)

Proving Your Mettle

Okay, so you don't know about the worst disaster to happen in weeks. That's pretty bad. However, you can partially recover your equilibrium, perhaps your dignity, by proving you have some knowledge on *another* news story. This way people will think you may have a weird lapse in your cultural awareness, but you are not an idiot.

After the initial fervor of the mudslide conversation dies down (and after having admitted you know nothing about it) you say something like, "That's what happens when you don't read the paper for a several days. But say, did you happen to read the amazing story in the *Times* a few weeks ago?" And then you proceed with what must be a very interesting news story—one that you *do* know.

I had a story I used to use in this situation. It was a story I had read in the *New York Times Magazine* about a biotech company in

Montreal that was adding spider genes to goat DNA. The resulting goats were able to produce a unique protein in their milk, and that milk was then used to make fibers for bulletproof vests. I had been so fascinated by the story that I remembered small details—for instance, that the resulting goats were only one-seventy-thousandth part spider, but even that small amount of arachnid genetic material was enough to put spiderweb capability in the goats' milk (!), and that the fiber would have a tensile strength of 300,000 pounds per square inch.

If you can lead the conversation around to a story like that—a story which is not only unusual and fascinating but about which you can remember intricate details—it works really well as an embarrassment salve. Your story has to be fairly recent in order for you to toss it into the conversation, and it's important for this face-saving routine that you know the story, whatever it is, in depth. This shows you are not a lightweight, and that, in spite of your being oblivious to the mudslide, you do know how to read a newspaper. Also, it introduces a new topic to the group.

High-Voltage Area! Talking Politics

We've all heard the old adage a million times: Never talk politics or religion. Our mothers drummed it into our heads (at least mine did), as did their mothers with them. The assumption is that these are two areas people feel very strongly about and they aren't subject to normal rules of logic and pleasant debate. People tend to disagree, especially when it comes to politics, in a more disagreeable manner than they do at any other time. Most people will admit that while a difference of opinion can be stimulating, yelling and name-calling can really wreck a party.

Also, when you are at a large party, you are supposed to be having conversations that are brief and plentiful. Once you start talking about next year's election, you're liable to forget all about circulating. But by far the most serious danger is the emotional one; most people, when talking politics, reach their boiling point quickly and find themselves saying things they hadn't planned on saying. When two or more guests start arguing, it can cause a kind of air bubble at the party; people nearby will turn and stare, or worse, join in—and then your discussion can interfere in everyone's mingling pleasure. (Like the time my friend's uncle Henry ruined the Christmas party when he got into a political argument and threw the turkey leg at his brother, yelling that bird brains should stick together.)

The dangers of talking politics are more prevalent than ever before, because issues in our country have become more and more polarized. Increasingly, there seems to be no middle ground. At my family gatherings we used to have spirited discussions about politics; we now never talk about it. Everyone knows it's like lighting a match in a house full of explosives. The trouble is that, even though now we don't fight, our conversations tend to be less interesting.

In Victorian days, every gentleman or gentlewoman learned the two safe topics for polite conversation: the weather and *your* health. Now even these once-benign areas are doorways to talking politics: the hot topic of global warming is a hop, skip, and a jump from an innocent comment about how warm the weather has been recently, and a courteous inquiry about someone's health can easily become a debate about the health care system. An innocent remark about someone's new fur hat or the Columbus Day parade can slide you right into politics before you can say "cheese and crackers."

The truth is there is hardly any way to really avoid talking politics. So, although mingling is for the most part supposed to be a lighthearted affair, mingling in the twenty-first century is bound to be a little less superficial. After all, what would be the point of mingling if all we ever talked about was the temperature and pungency of the tea? Our lives are too closely connected with politics to avoid the subject entirely. How can intelligent people gathered together for conversation totally avoid touching on foreign policy, congressional activities, oil policies, or homeland security issues? I believe it's about time we rewrote the time-honored golden rule to read: It's fine to talk politics and religion, just *don't argue violently about politics and religion.*

Talking politics has its minefields, but it can be worth it for the interesting conversations you can end up having. However, you do have to know how to negotiate your way through the dangers. (I am not going to differentiate between religion and politics because they have become so closely intertwined.)

1. **Know your own boiling point.** This is extremely important. You have to be certain that you can recognize that moment when you are about to go over the edge into anger—a very hard thing to pinpoint when you are in the middle of talking about nuclear proliferation—and stop. It's a bit like trying to stop drinking before you get drunk; when the moment comes, you can't relate to why you were determined to stop in the first place. If you don't think you

can do this (or if all your friends tell you you can't) then go back to the original rule. Don't talk politics.

2. **Test for friend, foe, or fanatic.** Even if you are capable in most circumstances of keeping your head, you have to be very careful with whom you talk politics. While it takes two to argue, I don't know many people who can stay serene when confronted with a fanatic. These days a lot of people will fall into that category. To help you spot one before it's too late, you should develop some test questions to administer to the person. These are designed to let you know if (a) you are talking to someone who is more or less in the same camp as you, (b) you are talking to someone from the other side who seems open-minded, and with whom you might be able to have an interesting debate, or (c) you are talking to someone who might become belligerent. Obviously you have to find the right moment for your test question so it does not seem to come out of nowhere. From his reaction you can decide if you think the water is safe. Keep a close watch on facial expression and body language; it can often tell you more than verbal response. The test lines below are just suggestions; this testing device, more than any other, requires your own personal touch. Warning: These kinds of tests are never foolproof. People's belief systems are not always as straightforward as you expect them to be.

"Did you happen to see the Huffington Post/Wall Street Journal *today?*
(If the person replies with a simple yes or no, they can be either liberal or conservative but probably not fanatically. If,

however, the person answers something like, "I never read that piece of crap, ever," he is most likely an extremist.)

"I just bumped into someone who looked exactly like [name of current political figure]."
(Example of fanatical responses: "I hope you hurt him." "I feel sorry for anyone who looks like him.")

"I always wonder why blue is for Democrats and red is for Republicans."
(Examples of fanatical responses: "Blue means sad, so blue must be because of all the stupid crying and whining the liberals do." "Red is for all the blood on their hands.")

3. **Be a diplomat.** Imagine that you're a foreign diplomat at an international cocktail party. Try to remain impersonal and cool, with observations such as "Our economy sure isn't doing too well now," rather than "Are you trying to tell me that we're not in desperate trouble economically?!" A good rule of thumb is to avoid asking questions about politics (unless they are truly informational, such as "Have you read about the bill Congress just passed?"), and don't let your voice get any louder or faster than it would be if you were talking about the glazed ham.

4. **Learn how to defuse and escape.** The minute you feel yourself losing control, or when you realize your partner in the political dispute has lost it, *defuse and/or escape*. This is not beginner stuff. Once again, you have to *want* to stop. (Breathing deeply may help, as will moving to another

place in the room, or getting somebody else to join both of you. Remember, *change equals movement; movement equals change*.) Here are some examples of lines you can use either to defuse the situation and go on talking about something else (not that likely, if one of you is in emotional overdrive) or to defuse and escape:

"Well, I don't know about that, but there's one thing I do know about: I'm starving! Will you excuse me?"

"Well, I guess we can't solve the world's problems in one night."

"Listen to us arguing! No wonder my mother always told me never to talk politics at a party! Do you want to get a drink?"

(Jokingly) *"Well, I guess we'd better either talk about something else or step outside!"*

The most important thing to remember when you decide to talk politics is your mingling objective (the one that should always override all others): You are there to have a good time, not to solve the world's problems or change anybody's mind (which you can't do anyway). So, shake hands and come out *not* fighting.

AHOY POLLOI: MINGLING IN PUBLIC PLACES

Ignoring the early training of childhood, I make a habit of talking to strangers whenever I am out in public. Not all mingling is done at parties. You never know what interesting people you may meet if you just take the initiative.

Years ago I attended a Pavarotti concert in Central Park. I was supposed to meet up with some friends who had gotten there several hours in advance. Unfortunately I had misjudged how large the crowd would be; by the time I got there it was wall-to-wall blankets, with hardly any space to squeeze through. As I tried to move forward through the sea of people, I was met with annoyed comments at every turn. I realized that everyone thought I was just trying to get a space closer to the stage—in other words, jump the line. What with the thickness of the crowd and the mood of the audience, I knew I was going to have a hard time getting to my friends. (This was before cell phones; today I could have at least obtained some coordinates.)

Luckily, I had with me two delicious, homemade apple pies. I began by stopping and sharing a small piece of my pie with a couple of women closest to me. I chatted with them awhile, then moved on to another group of people; I soon gave some-one else a taste of pie. People were jammed so close together that the word spread that someone was giving away pie. I used my piece-of-pie offering, along with some serious mingling, to keep moving forward. I was able to explain, along the way, that I had friends up ahead who were saving a place for me. I met numerous people that day and had a grand time. I finally did manage to reach my friends, although all I had left of the pie were the empty boxes!

Next time you're stuck in a crowd, waiting in line, or just hanging out at a café, hit the schmooze button. Even if you happen to be pie-less.

Mingling Outdoors or in a Crowd

There are times when we are by ourselves at outdoor concerts, airports, train stations, bus stations, amusement parks, sporting events, beaches, parades, fireworks displays, shopping malls, theater lobbies, auditoriums, or Herald Square at Christmas time. You're there anyway so why not mingle a little? Mingling in these situations is very much like mingling in a crowded party (see The Sardine Can, page 199), except, of course, since you are out in public, you will find that people will feel more vulnerable and therefore will be a little more cautious. Here are some tips:

- **Ask for help:** Ask people for directions, for advice, or for information. Most people are happy to be of service, and you could end up having a nice time in addition to getting the information you need. Once I was trying to get from Manhattan's Upper West Side to Brooklyn on the subway, but due to track work, there were confusing and complicated "service changes" (transit speak for "Just forget it; it's impossible to get there right now"). I was totally flummoxed—and, of course, I was late. After a few frantic moments, I spotted a friendly looking couple to ask for advice. It turned out that they were on their way to the same neighborhood! I traveled with them all the way (we had to transfer several times). We had a wonderful talk; I interviewed them for this book and we exchanged numbers. The subway trip was like a fun party, and the experience left me with a definite post-mingle glow. It wouldn't have happened if I hadn't decided to ask strangers for help.

- **Commiserate:** Complain about the train that's broken down, about how long the band is taking to start up, how loud the music is, how you hate being on jury duty, how many jellyfish are in the water, or how noisy or hot it is. Misery absolutely adores company.

- **Form a Tribe:** If you manage to find a few like-minded people nearby, form a little group and hang out for the duration. If you have a dog or a kid with you, it is super easy to talk to other people who also have dogs or kids. Remember, with the right attitude you can make a party anywhere.

That's My Queue: Lines in Line

The average person spends two to three years of her life waiting in line: checkout lines, bank lines, ticket lines, restaurant lines, and the most daunting and torturous line of all: the ubiquitous line for the ladies' room. Long lines can be tiring, frustrating, and boring—a real waste of time. But they don't have to be. Because almost every one of those tedious experiences can be turned into a socializing situation.

Think about it. You've got all those people, standing together not talking to one another, for the most part; and they already have one thing in common: whatever it is you are standing in line for. That's more of a beginning than you have at many parties, where sometimes the only thing you have in common is the host. Many people immediately whip out their cell phones to pass the time; why not look around you instead and see what happens?

I would not say that mingling while on line is easy; there

are many obstacles, not least being the very fact of the line itself. You are basically trying to mingle without the use of your legs. Many techniques—escape, for example—are drastically different when you are in a line. You have to overcome people's natural suspicion of you (a lot of people are uncomfortable if a stranger starts talking to them), plus you must be prepared for your conversation to be overheard by the entire line. When you mingle in a line, you are usually conversing directly with only one or two people, but you are almost *performing* for a large group—who feel no compunction about standing around eavesdropping, and anyway they can't very much help it, can they? And I for one would rather listen to two people talking behind me than someone talking on their phone.

People can be loathe to get into a conversation with you in these situations, because they know if it's unpleasant in any way it is almost impossible to make the conversation stop. You can't very well excuse yourself and go get a drink. People have the same squeamishness standing in line as they do about talking to their seatmate on a plane. But you are stuck there, and you may as well try. Remember, it's not all that different from a sit-down dinner situation; if you don't like the person on one side of you, try the other one. Note: This is another arena where it is completely acceptable to complain. Commiserate about the length of the line or about the shameless woman you just saw cutting in up ahead.

Mingling in lines can be rewarding, and because you will probably never see any of these people again (famous last words!), it's relatively risk-free. Here are some specific rules and sample lines for the various on-line mingles (an * signifies that the line is generic; it can be used for any of the following line situations):

Checkout lines: People in checkout lines can be tough customers, depending on what they are buying. Many people put on their personal armor when they are about to purchase something. If what they've got in their basket or cart looks a bit strange or personal to you, don't mention it. You're going to have to be very nonthreatening and incredibly nice when you deliver your opening line. Be sure to smile wider and more often than you might normally.

In most checkout lines (like those in grocery stores) you are strictly limited to the person in front of you and the person behind you. If all the lines are long and you have a choice, why not choose the line that has the most interesting-looking people in it rather than the one that is going to get you out five minutes faster?

Here are some possible lines for when you are checking out:

"Oh, I love that stuff."

"It looks like you're having a party."

"Are you going to carry all that yourself? Wow!"

"Is this the express line?"

*"Have you been waiting long?"**

*"Do you ever wonder how much of our lives is spent in lines?"** *(Especially good at the post office.)*

Ticket, restaurant, and movie lines: Waiting in line for an event is a good place to mingle, as you are waiting in line for something pleasurable. People are usually in an excited, anticipatory mood—or everyone is feeling impatient. A word of caution here: Most people don't like to hear other people complain about having to wait in line ("How much longer is it going to be, why don't they let us in!") unless the comment is witty, or funny, or meant to inspire a sense of camaraderie. Always remember, unless you are dealing with the Truly Arrogant, conversation while mingling should be good-natured. Some sample lines are:

"Have you heard good things about [name of the movie or restaurant]?"

"Have you guys been here before?"

"I always feel funny, standing in these lines by myself!"

"This better be worth it!"

Ladies' room lines: This is by far the easiest line in which to mingle. Women standing in the seemingly endless, inevitable line for the ladies' room bond together with only the slightest encouragement, because all of them are equally exasperated at having to stand in line to go to the bathroom and probably miss the beginning of the second act as they always do. I've met some great people in ladies' room lines, but I find the conversation doesn't vary much. In fact, what I do in ladies' room lines is sometimes more like organizing a revolt than mingling. Try these lines:

"When I become president, I'm going to revamp women's rooms throughout the nation."

"Ten more minutes of this and I'm hitting the men's room."

"They want a definition of Purgatory? This is it."

"If men all had to stand in line to go to the bathroom, for just one month, it would change the world forever."

Please note: Bank lines are not good places for talking to strangers; people are usually too anxious about taking care of business.

Elevator Mingling

I have always found it disturbing that people seem to have trouble talking to each other in elevators. We enter this little room, stand close together, stare tensely at the display panel— or, more and more common these days, the "incidental video screen" you are forced to watch—and breathe a sigh of relief when we get out. Most people tell me there's a good reason for this behavior: Our personal space is so infringed upon that our barriers are up. That's reasonable; after all, it is a very small space to be standing in. But if you think about it, you are standing no closer to people than you are at a crowded party. The difference is that you are in a tiny room that moves and does not seem altogether safe. Everyone is mildly anxious. It's a transitional experience, and people just want it to be over. Well, why not mingle away that anxiety?

We should get over our elevator stiffness and take advantage of these golden opportunities (however brief they may be) to interact. I believe people are secretly desperate to learn how to elevate their elevator time. So if you're ready for new frontiers, here are the rules:

1. **Say hello.** It's polite to greet everyone in the elevator as you enter, and also to greet people who get on after you. You'll be surprised at how people will warm up to this. Always accompany your salutation with a smile (your smile will have to be a bit more impersonal than one you would use at a party, especially if you are the only other person in the car—you don't want to scare anybody).

2. **Include the entire elevator in your conversation.** If you are getting into the elevator with someone else, or you discover someone you know in the elevator, don't ignore the others present. This will be a challenge for most, as people have always found it acceptable to have a conversation with another person almost as if there weren't four other people standing right next to them! I have always thought this behavior bizarre and alienating, and it's time it stopped. Your attitude should be that you and your friend have just joined a new group of people at a party. Turn toward the people already in the elevator (only slightly—most people who haven't caught on yet to the proper social behavior in elevators will all be facing front, so your turn must be gentle). Make brief eye contact with people—as you greet them

and then once in a while during conversation—but only for a microsecond. The smaller and more crowded the elevator, the less eye contact you should make.

3. **Never make jokes about the elevator breaking down.**
It's helpful to use humor to dispel the tension that exists in any elevator situation, and it is tempting to joke about cable breaks and electronic failures, but *don't do it*. It may get a nervous laugh out of most people, but it could push the claustrophobic right over the edge.

4. **Talk about:** The sluggishness of the elevator, the décor inside, what's on the video screen, the doorman of the building, if there is one. Also, if you are in an apartment building, you can comment on someone's mail (not personal mail, but magazines you happen to spot). For example, I once took a long elevator ride with someone who was carrying a copy of a computer magazine; we had a very nice chat about the best kind of scanner to buy. Elevator rides are, for the most part, short, so don't forget to begin your mingling when you are waiting for the elevator (heaven knows, that could increase your mingling time to fifteen minutes). Here are some lines to help you get started:

"Excuse me, but do you work [live] in this building? I haven't seen you before."

"Is there a thirteenth floor in this building? No? Is that a way of dating the building?"

"We've all got to stop meeting like this."

"Do you lose your stomach [Do your ears pop] in elevators or is it just me?"

As usual, these lines are not to everyone's taste. You may want to start a conversation by simply saying "Nice weather we're having." The point is, whether you are stuck in an elevator with two other people or you are in Disney World with two thousand, do not miss the chance to connect with the people around you. Work your mingling magic and you never know who you may meet.

THE BUSINESS OF MINGLING FOR BUSINESS

As I said in the beginning of this book, the techniques for business mingling are basically the same as for any other kind of mingling. The best socializing is achieved by not putting your networking agenda first. However, there are some things to keep in mind when you are at a professional function or business setting, whether it be your company-wide holiday party, an industry convention, or a party to entertain clients. You will have the best success if you try *not* to talk about work, at least not overtly. If you want to make lasting connections, talk about other things, get to know the people as people first, at least for five or ten minutes. Don't start talking about your position, accomplishments, or career goals. The better you get to know the person outside his business role, the more likely it is that whatever business relationship you have or want to have will work better. "Which department are you in?" does not telegraph to the other person that they are about to have an interesting conversation.

When you are mingling for business purposes, it will also benefit you to become a bit of a mingling paragon. Upon your arrival tell the host how well he is looking and how much you have been looking forward to coming. Exude goodwill. Smile at everyone. Adopt a kid-in-a-candy-shop air. Introduce yourself as much as possible, and then introduce people you know or have met to each other. If someone makes a joke that doesn't go over, do your part to try to smooth things over for him. Offer to help whenever and wherever there is an opportunity. Assist others in making connections as you make connections yourself. Positive energy is always important in mingling, but in most business affairs, it's paramount.

If it's your own interoffice party be sure not to sit around talking to people you already know. And though it's obvious I'm going to say it anyway: Too much booze, you lose.

Name-Tag Tips

I went through a period in my life when I refused to wear the sticky, annoying labels we are all requested to don at many business, pseudo-business, alumnae, church, or association affairs. After all, if you're wearing a bright blue or red tag that announces "HELLO MY NAME IS _____," you can feel ridiculous saying it as well; it's almost as if you're reading your name tag aloud to the other person. I used to have this nightmarish fantasy that someone would yell back at me, "Yes, I know, I can read!"

I've mellowed on the subject of name tags since then. Now

I believe you should wear them if they are provided, with the exception of the ones that pin on. (Call me fussy, but I don't think anyone should be asked to poke holes in their clothing in the name of socializing, unless they're wearing burlap.) Even though name tags are a silly mingling crutch, I have found that it is better to go ahead and wear them, if for no other reason than it makes you part of the group. Also, you never know, someone at the party may have been told to talk to you because you're fabulous or brilliant (or available!), and that person may be darting in and out of clusters of people, scoping out tags, hoping to find you. If you are not wearing a name tag, you could miss the best conversation of your night.

However, if you are bored by the prospect of conventional name-tag practice, and, more important, you know you are with a playful group, here are some suggestions to liven things up:

• **Wear it in an interesting place.** I've seen tags on lapels (sideways), purses or briefcases, hats, the lower part of a jacket, even sleeves. Women sometimes choose an alternative to the chest because they feel uncomfortable having people look pointedly at that part of their body. As long as you have elected to wear a name tag, you may as well get the most out of it conversationally. And if your tag is in an interesting, even original, place, it can be an icebreaker. However, you don't want to make it *too* hard to read or it defeats the whole purpose.

• **Write something else instead of your name.** This is admittedly kind of silly, but hey, depending on what field you are in, you may have colleagues who like silly. You could write something like "Guess Who?" or maybe "Don't you hate name tags?" I've even heard of taping on a bar code in place of a name. You'd be surprised how many people enjoy seeing something out of the ordinary. Caution: Don't go too far. Never, ever write something that is crude or impolite in any way (this includes remarks that are sexist, racist, etc.). If you have to ask yourself "Is this offensive?," don't do it.

- **Use punctuation.** A question mark or exclamation point after your name may be a fun choice for quirky crowds. Emoticons? If you can't resist a smiley face go ahead.

Of course, many times the name tag is preprinted. But whether or not you can and do use any of the above unsubtle name-tag enhancements, there are a couple of things to keep in mind when mingling among name-tag wearers. If you are going with the straight name-tag approach, be sure to write clearly in large letters so that people don't have to stick their faces close to your chest to read your name. Also, it's best not to look at a person's tag until you have approached him or the group he is in. It's very ill-mannered to be seen checking out the tags of everyone in the room unless you can appear to be on a dedicated mission looking for someone specific. If you do glance at people's tags while you pass by, do not make eye contact with any of them, or it will be as if you are saying, "I don't like your name, I don't like your face; I'm going to look elsewhere for conversational partners." Also, when you enter into a conversation with someone, it's best to be definite with regard to the tag; either look at it and comment on it, or don't look at it (at least not so they notice).

A great name-tag trick is to glance quickly at the tag without letting the wearer see you. Then wait a few minutes and slip the wearer's name into the conversation as if you're old chums ("Well, Keith . . ."). This simple trick, when done well, will make the other person feel good. It's the most amazing thing that a person can be in a whole room of people wearing name tags, and yet forget he has one on himself.

Business Card Advice

In their professional life, people still use real live business cards (although there are now phone apps like Evernote, which allow you to scan the card directly into your phone). It's still quicker to whip out your card and hand it to someone than it is to enter information into your smartphone.

Time it right: Offer your card when your conversation is winding down and you sense the other person is about to move on to another group, or you are. I believe it is better etiquette, as it is less aggressive, to offer your own card up instead of requesting hers. Most likely she will automatically give you hers in return, but this allows her the option not to. And you never want to be in the position of asking someone for her card, and have her say, "I'm so sorry, I only brought a few." You can also wait until the very end of the party, get your card ready and go back to the contact to say good-bye for the night, and add, "By the way, here's my card." But of course you risk the person leaving before you can do this.

Make notes: Right after you've talked to someone whose given you his business card—or if that is too awkward, immediately upon leaving the party—make some notes on the back of the card to remind you where you met him and the nature of the conversation you had. It might be a restaurant you talked about, a new website, or sending your kids to college. Even a scrawled word or two will help you put a face to the name days later, and this will also enhance the quality of your follow-up email or text. Specific references will serve you well; the person will feel that you really remembered him and enjoyed the conversation, and that you are not just contacting him because you found his card in your wallet along with twenty others.

MINGLING FOR LOVE

There is really no secret at all to mingling for love. Again, it requires the same skills and attitude as any other kind of socializing, except you may want to use flirtier lines and have lower lighting.

One day I was talking to my single friend Sue. She had been to a party the night before.

"So did you mingle?" (I always ask this of my friends, I can't help it. I've got mingling on the brain.)

"There were no single men there," answered Sue.

"That's too bad. But did you mingle?"

"There *weren't* any men, I told you!"

"But did you *mingle?*" I persisted. At last she got my meaning.

"Oh, well, yes, of course. In fact, I met this really interesting woman in my business . . ."

Mingling is mingling. (And online dating notwithstanding, sometimes love is what happens to us when we are busy doing something else.) You never know where your "dream" man or woman is going to come from; it could end up being the brother or sister of someone you meet at tonight's party. The more connections you make, the better your chances are for finding a mate—and the better is it for your life in general.

Let me put it another way: Imagine that you knew you were going to meet the love of your life two years from now. What would you do in the meantime? What most people would do is just enjoy life to the fullest, pursuing the things you love, meeting people whenever there is an opportunity, and this is what you should do, too.

On the other hand, it won't hurt to go over a few basics for the single-minded:

Nonparty Love Venues

Here are a few tips for doing the single-mingle in particular settings other than at a party:

- **Bars and restaurants:** I've heard of restaurants where it is completely dark and you can't see the food (where this is done on purpose, I mean); I've been to bars where the music is so loud that flirting is frankly an impossibility without cue cards. If you are looking for sex, and think conversation is old-fashioned, then a sensory-deprived atmosphere may be fine. But I believe if you are looking for a romantic relationship, you should make a habit of hanging out at places that have soft-ish lighting and soft-ish music. Otherwise you may not even notice when someone is making advances. Warning: It's almost impossible not to stare into your phone when you are in a bar and are nervous, but if you are looking for love you should keep your phone use to a minimum. In decades past you might have smoked a cigarette. The difference is, with a cigarette you could still make eye contact with a love interest, which you can't do if you are texting. On the other hand, I know a woman who always brings a book with her ("Dudes love to ask me what I'm reading!").

Most pickup lines are too horrible to talk about. I find the best kind of approach in a bar or a restaurant is the commiseration/plea for assistance, such as:

"I bet the bar in Hell is like this. You can see the bartender but he can't see you."

"I wish they'd turn up the music. I think there are some people in the next state who can't hear it."

"Excuse me, have you seen a tall man with a red beard [woman with a yellow jacket]? I was supposed to meet a friend and I'm afraid he [she] may not be coming."

However, if you like a more provocative line, you might try one of these:

"If you are married or gay [straight] I swear I'll kill myself."

"So where've I been all your life, anyway?"

"I usually don't talk to strange men [women] but you don't look too strange."

- **Stores:** Stores are excellent places for talking to strangers, so why couldn't you find romance? Since everyone is looking at the same merchandise, you already have something in common. You can't always trust the salespeople, so it's quite natural to ask opinions of your fellow shoppers. If you are a woman looking for a man, a computer store is especially fruitful; there you are, amidst all that daunting manly technology and hardware—no wonder you want company and comfort! I once chatted up five or six men at Best Buy when I was shopping for a new laptop. In a clothing store, you can ask other people's opinion of what you are thinking of buying ("Does this look okay?"). If you are a man looking for a woman, there's always the corny: "Pardon me, but I need a woman (laugh) . . . I mean, I need a woman's *opinion* on this."

  Home Depot and other similar mega stores are great for pickups; in the vast alienating universe of Costco or Ikea, who wouldn't want to reach out to talk to strangers? Housewares stores are especially good because you can communicate the fact of your singlehood fairly quickly during your conversation about the linoleum tiles or bath mats.

- **Museums:** Museums are trickier; while many people are there alone and might not mind company, there are some people who simply want to enjoy the peace and quiet and solitude of the art. You do, of course, have all the subject matter you need right up there on the walls, but remember, keep your voice low and your cell phone off. Try a line like, "Those aren't really Georgia O'Keeffe's hands in that painting,

are they?" Or, "Excuse me, but I find this piece so disturbing; does it affect you the same way?"

Romance Copilots

Looking for romance can be so daunting that many people
will take a companion along to the party for moral support.
In this case there are two choices: You can go to the party
with another person who is looking for love, or you can take
a wingman.

Wingmen or wingwomen (also known as "pivots") are platonic friends you take along to help you mingle for love. Many
people find it is easier to meet a love interest when they have
an ally at their side. These accomplices can provide cover for you,
as well as an entrée; they can act as buffers, scouts, prescreeners,
and shills when you are approaching romantic prospects. If after
talking to a prospect for five or ten minutes you decide you
aren't interested, your wing can act the part of your mate (if he
or she is the appropriate sex) and give you an easy out. If, on
the other hand, you *are* attracted to the person, your wing can
help you stay level-headed and make sure it's safe and advisable
for you to proceed. Wings can help get information, as well as
promote you to the prospect.

The other option is taking a fellow romance seeker along.
This can be very comforting; your friend is in the same emotional place you are, and it's fun to compare notes. However,
be sure you don't end up competing for the same romantic
prospect. It's usually not worth ending your friendship over. I
know all's fair in love and all that, but if possible you should
try not to get in the way of your friend's game. Women deal
with this by talking to each other in advance of approaching a

man ("I've got dibs on that tall guy with the tattoo!"); frankly, I've never been able to discover *how* men deal with it. They probably go off in a corner and do rock-paper-scissors.

Always remember, whether you are mingling at a nightclub, a health club, a self-help workshop, a convention, a church social, or a good old-fashioned cocktail party, try not to limit your mingling to potential dates. Your aim should always be to meet as many people as possible. Of course, there's no rule against going back to have a second or third chat with someone you're attracted to. But unless you fall madly in love, circulate. He or she will be more intrigued if you don't cling.

If you *should* happen to meet your soul mate, and fall in love at first sight, complete with bells ringing and spine shivers, by all means . . . stop mingling for the night.

HOSTING: HOW TO PLEASE YOUR GUESTS EVERY TIME

The best hostess story I ever heard was about a dinner party during which one of the guests, who had had a little too much to drink, knocked over a full glass of red wine onto the table. The table was covered in a fine white linen tablecloth, and what made the incident even worse was that the employer of both the hostess and the tipsy guest was present. There was a moment of stunned silence and then, quick as a flash, the hostess made a sudden, sweeping motion with her hand, knocking over her own glass of wine. "Look how clumsy we all are tonight," she laughed, completely saving the day for the abashed guest. Not many hosts will go quite that far to put their guests at ease. Frequently it's the host herself who is a nervous wreck.

Host Phobia

Right before I'm about to give a party I usually get a queasy feeling in my stomach. This sensation is not caused by sampling too much dip, or being nervous at the prospect of seeing a potential beau. No, this is the uneasy feeling that is born solely of the mortifying memories of parties past.

There was that horrible time I messed up the invitations and managed to invite both the current and the ex-boyfriend of my friend Patty (the ex-boyfriend drank too much gin and wouldn't leave). Then there was the time I prepared for a cocktail party for fifty and only eleven showed up—and that included the neighbor who I shanghaied at the last minute to try to fill the room. There was the big birthday bash I'd planned weeks in advance, and then at the last minute I was sequestered on a jury, of all things, and had to host the party with two armed guards by my side. Of course I'll never forget the party during which one of my guests (a would-be writer) kept going up to everyone else there and saying, "Do *you* want to be my agent?"

When you decide to host any kind of party you are asking for it. But if you're like me, you'll risk just about anything for the wonderful energy you get (not the anxiety, but that *other* feeling) from having a collection of friends gathered together in your home. No matter what else happens, I always try to emulate the famous hostess Elsa Maxwell, who with only three words always made sure her guests felt welcome: "When they arrive," she is quoted as saying, "I murmur, 'At last,' and when they arise to depart I protest, 'Already?'"

Above all, enjoy your hosthood. If you are having a good time, chances are your guests will, too.

The Party Coach

We all know people who are fabulous hosts or hostesses: people whose parties you never want to miss, and whose houses you never want to leave. What makes them such good hosts? Simple. They do more than open their doors and provide food. They make certain that everyone has a good time.

Any self-respecting host should make sure that his guests are in fact mingling, and that no one is left standing morosely off in a corner by him- or herself. The host is, in effect, the mingling coach for the evening, and that makes it his responsibility to see that people are mixing. Basically, what the host does throughout the entire night is similar to the Human Sacrifice escape technique, except that it is for more altruistic purposes. He talks to someone for a few minutes, then leads that person over to someone else. A good host doesn't then merely introduce the two people, he offers them something they have in common; in other words, he provides them with their first bit of subject matter, just to get things moving. Then he's off, to do the same thing again for two or three other people he has spotted who aren't talking to each other. Any conversational "singles," be they the Shy Wallflowers or the Obnoxious Ones everyone else at the party is trying to get away from, must be "married" by the conscientious host—even drunks and bores (the host who's really on the ball will match these kinds up together). Has a minglephobe come to the party? A clever host will offer him a job to do; he will get him to pass food, hang coats, pour drinks, or man the music, and he will make sure the minglephobe is busy with tasks that necessitate his interacting with people.

Certainly it's okay for a host to have a little selfish mingle of his own now and then that has nothing to do with helping anybody else have a good time. But the host's personal conversation time per group should be shorter than if he were a guest, and he must make sure he spends a few moments, no matter how brief, with every single person who sets foot in his home. (Even if it's somebody's cousin who wasn't even invited.) It helps, of course, that a host has no need of exit lines; the mere fact of his being host will allow him to say "Excuse me" graciously at any time during any conversation. Everyone understands the duties of a host. However, the party giver's real enjoyment should come from watching his own hostly handiwork: the knitting of his friends or colleagues together.

Note: It goes without saying (but I'm going to say it anyway) that no host should ever become excessively inebriated. In addition to the many obvious reasons for this, being a host is a major responsibility, like being mother and father to the whole party. You definitely need all your faculties intact.

The Feng Shui of Hosting

If you want to create a good and healthy party flow, here are some tips, loosely based on the principles of Feng Shui:

If space will allow it, place the bar area at one end of the room and the food at the other. That way people will be forced to move back and forth, and it will do a lot to promote mingling.

Or place the bar and the food table in different rooms. The more people have to move around to get what they need the more kinetic your party will be. (Even better is if you can manage to have maneuvering room around the food table.) If possible, the food and/or bar, as well as most of the places to sit, should be opposite from the doorways.

An inspired host may want to create what I like to call a "party heart." If you've invited a lot of people who don't know each other, it is helpful to give your guests a central area around which to gather. Mostly people use the food table for their focal point, but there are other options. I was reminded of this hosting tip at a recent party where the host had cleverly arranged things so that his computer (with Pandora on it) was accessible to everyone in the kitchen. (His was a large kitchen with a center island.) Everyone clustered around, scrolling through the music selection, talking about their favorite music, picking out tunes. It gave guests a common focal point and a place to keep coming back to. Watching people's faces bathed in the blue light of the computer screen, I felt as if there were a hearth fire by which everyone was warming themselves.

Note: In my opinion, the lighting and the music are both very important. For everyone to feel relaxed and comfortable, you need indirect lighting and music that is not so loud that you have to shout to be heard. If you have overhead light fixtures—that is, light coming directly from the ceiling—try to make sure those are turned off. When my readers protest, "But I want people to really *see* each other," I say to them what Blanche DuBois said in *A Streetcar Named Desire*: "I don't want reality, I want magic!"

7

Handling Difficult Situations

LIE OR DIE

Let's say you have memorized fifty brilliant opening lines, and that you have all the right props; let's say you have even mastered the Butterfly Flit. Now you're an expert in the art of mingling, right? Not necessarily. The true test of whether you are a good mingler lies not in what you do under normal circumstances but in what you do in an emergency. Being able to handle yourself well in unexpected or unusual mingling situations takes concentration, imagination, flexibility, and—by far the most important ingredient—the unhesitating, unwavering ability to lie *through your teeth*. I can't stress enough how important the white lie is in mingling, especially when you are faced with imminent disaster of some kind. It can be absolutely essential to your survival. Remember, you're on the mingling battlefield, facing impossible odds, fierce opposition, near calamity. You never know what you'll be asked to handle. While your course of action may or may not call for a friendly fib, it's important to know from the start that when the moment of truth arrives, you may have to . . . lie or die.

DEALING WITH FAUX PAS

You are at an art gallery opening; your escort is a close friend of the artist whose work is being shown. After mingling for over an hour with various groups of people, you return to talk to a woman with whom you have chatted previously but to whom you have not been formally introduced. You remark to her that while you find the paintings somewhat interesting, you don't really "get what it's all about." Then you ask her, "So, are you an artist, too?" She responds somewhat coolly, "Actually, this is *my* opening."

We've all made embarrassing errors while mingling; I have made some real doozies myself. And yet, each time it happens, each time we're faced with that excruciating moment right after the faux pas when we wish we could just disappear into the floorboards, we're convinced that no one has ever been so stupid or so clumsy before.

How many times has the following happened to you?

- Calling someone you know by the wrong name
- Being overheard gossiping by the person who is the object of the gossip
- Bumping into someone or spilling something on someone

- Bringing up a subject you immediately realize had been a secret
- Talking about last night's great party to which persons present weren't invited
- Mistaking someone's wife or husband for their daughter or son
- Asking a nonexpectant woman about her pregnancy
- Broaching a taboo topic of conversation

Whether you've just stepped on someone's foot with your spiked heel or inquired as to the whereabouts of someone's dead husband, try to remember two things: Everyone makes faux pas, even the person to whom you've just done the damage; and there's always a way to recover (at least partially) from any snafu, and to make the best of a bad situation. The important thing is not to fold under the pressure of your social blunder, but instead deal with it and learn from it. Faux pas build mingling character, and if you don't run away from them, they can help to make you a much stronger conversationalist. Just think of it as you would a dance. Even though every once in a while you may falter, you don't stop dancing. As Al Pacino says in *Scent of a Woman,* "If you make a mistake, get all tangled up, just tango on!"

When You're Dressed Wrong

If you've ever walked into a room full of tuxedos and evening gowns in a tweed skirt and knee-highs, as I have, you have experienced the particular vise of horror that grips you when you realize you're dressed all wrong for the party. I'm not talking here about having on a turtleneck instead of a tie; I mean when you are dressed noticeably, definitely *wrong*.

When you find yourself in this situation, you have several choices. Please note: I am assuming here that the fact that you're dressed wrong bothers you; naturally, if you are either confident enough or enlightened enough not to care, you won't think of this as a faux pas and the following advice doesn't apply.

You can, of course, leave. Turn right around and walk out, go get takeout, and spend a quiet night at home, convinced it was fate and you would have had a lousy time anyway. But I emphatically do not condone this course of action. It's giving up.

Your second option is to dash home and change into an appropriate outfit. If you think you can pull this off, by all means, go for it. But be sure to get out before anybody sees you, or your "Before" and "After" show might be more embarrassing than merely being dressed wrong. Also, the logistics of getting home, changing your clothes, and getting back to the party before it's over may be overwhelming. The stressfulness of all that running back and forth may not be worth it. It's bound to put you in a bad mood.

The third choice: Pretend nothing is wrong with the way you are dressed. In your mind you must see yourself dressed in completely appropriate clothing, then just mingle as you normally would. But don't forget what happened to the emperor in "The Emperor's New Clothes." All it takes is for one person to say to you, "Did you forget this was black tie?" and the illusion could be shattered.

Your fourth option: You can use humor, the universal antidote for faux pas. For instance, if you are in casual clothes and everyone else is in formal dress, you can say in mock amazement, "Look how many people are inappropriately dressed; imagine anyone wearing a tux to an affair like this!" As always with humor, it has to be funny; if you don't think you can pull it off, don't attempt it.

Your last option, and the one I *do* suggest you choose, is this: *Turn your inappropriate appearance into an interesting story.* This way, you take the hand that's been dealt to you and bluff it out. Imagine you arrive in a gray business suit and blue shirt at your friend Miranda's house and, upon entering, you realize everyone is in black tie except you. Suddenly you remember: The invitation *did* say formal, but you had such a bad day at the office it went right out of your head. But you don't panic. You know that before you begin to mingle, before you talk to anyone, all you have to do is take the time to decide what your story is going to be. You remain in the coatroom or foyer for a minute, until you are ready.

You confidently enter the fray. After your opening line, you indicate your attire and say laughingly, "Can you believe this? Miranda really got me this time. She neglected to inform me about it being black tie. I pulled the same trick on her two years ago and we've been paying each other back ever since." This leads you and the other person into a discussion of practical jokes and of how you both know the hostess. You've successfully turned your inappropriate dress into usable subject matter.

Admittedly, this is a rather bold lie, as it involves fabricating something untrue about the hostess. (It usually is not a good idea to tell lies about other people.) But Miranda, if she is a friend of yours, won't mind this innocent ruse, even if she does hear about it, which is highly unlikely. A less outrageous story might be that you have just gotten off a train or plane, and didn't have time to go home first. Or you can say that you've been locked out of your apartment, or that the cleaners burned down (along with all your dressy clothes), or that a jealous ex-lover has been stealing all your mail and you never received the actual invitation. Whatever tale you choose to tell, make it intriguing. Remember, your objective is not merely to recover from your fashion faux pas, but to make it work for you, to turn it into a mingling aid, just like wearing an accessory or bringing a prop.

As you can imagine, it's easier to pull this off if you are over-dressed rather than underdressed, like when you're wearing a tux and everyone else is in jeans. Then you simply adopt the position that you are going (or have already gone) to some very fancy, chic affair other than the present one.

A final note: Don't forget to consider telling the truth before you decide on a falsehood. But only if the truth is as interesting as a made-up story would be. If the truth is that you just made a stupid mistake for no particular reason, stick to deceit. This isn't Sunday school, this is a party!

Introductions: A Recurring Nightmare

The problem of being awkward with introductions is not unusual. In fact, 99.999 percent of us have some trouble in this area. You may be uncertain about whether to introduce someone using their first name, last name, or both; about whether to use a qualifier ("this is my accountant"); even about whether or not it is in fact your responsibility to introduce two people in a given situation. However, all of this is small potatoes compared with the seemingly inevitable mingling nightmare of having to introduce someone *whose name you have forgotten.*

Flubbing names during introductions is such a common faux pas that I have given this particular lack of social grace a clinical term: *dysnomnesia.* Dysnomnesia afflicts everyone at one time or another. Either you can't remember the person's name, you use an incorrect qualifier (such as "and this is her husband," when the two people are not married), or you actually start a conversation before you realize you have mistaken the person for someone else.

Whatever form your greeting goof takes, one thing is certain: The more important it is that you get it right, the more likely it is that you are going to screw up in some frightful way. So whether you've just forgotten your boss's name or your own, here are some recovery lines that may help to alleviate the situation:

> *"I'm so sorry; I have a name disorder called dysnomnesia. Really. I've been diagnosed by a name disorder specialist—Dr. . . . Dr. . . . I can't remember his name!"*

> *"I've never been able to remember names; it runs in my family. At family reunions there is generally a lot of 'Hey yous.' "*

> *"Whoops, I'm afraid I thought you were Bob Tompkins. Well, we were obviously meant to talk together. There are no accidents in life, right?"*

It's one thing to forget someone's name if you've met them only once or twice, or if you haven't seen them in a while. But all too often it's someone whose name you really should know, and who is going to be insulted to find out you don't. In other words, a faux pas in the making. This is absolute agony when it happens, and I've watched hundreds of minglers try to deal with it in different ways, ranging from exuberant apology ("Oh GOD, I'm so sorry, JEEZ, wow, I can't *believe* this, I can't *believe* I've forgotten your name!") to throwing up their hands and walking away. But there are better ways to deal with this kind of mental slip. Next time you draw a blank while making introductions, try one of the following ploys:

- **Manipulate them into introducing themselves.** This is the smoothest and most effective way to handle your memory lapse. When it's done well, no one will ever suspect you. If you have forgotten one person's name in the group, turn to that person first and smile. Then turn invitingly to a person whose name you *do* remember and say, "This is Tony Lopez," turning back casually toward the forgotten person. The person whose name you haven't mentioned yet will automatically (it's a reflex) say, "Nice to meet you, Tony, I'm Sylvia Cooper," and usually offer a hand to shake. If you are trying to introduce two people and you can't remember *either* of their names, your problem is more serious. Still, you can usually get away with simply saying, "Have you two met each other?" If you smile confidently and wait, the two will introduce themselves (though those few seconds while you're waiting can seem like a lifetime). At the very worst it will appear as if your introduction skills are a bit sloppy, but no one will be able to tell you've forgotten their names.

- **Confess, then dwell on it.** Here's another example of turning a faux pas to your advantage. What you do is admit you've forgotten the name(s), apologizing sincerely. After the introductions are over, let the mishap lead you into a discussion of why it is harder for some people to remember names than others (the left brain/right brain theory, the male/female theory, etc.). It may help you to keep in mind that almost everyone has a bad memory when it comes to names, and yet almost everyone thinks it's a unique failing. Using your own social error as subject matter shows that you are comfortable with your mistake; you don't feel that guilty about it. And since people tend to believe whatever you project, no one will hold a grudge.

- **Introduce them using something besides their name.** Names and labels are highly overrated in our society anyway. Why not say instead, "Jody, I want you to meet a woman after your own heart!" Then you just present the other person, who will offer her name or not. You can also cover up any uneasiness you have about forgetting names by using flattery: "I want you to meet the most fascinating person at the party!" or "You two should really meet—seeing as how you're both so gorgeous!" If you lay it on thick, it puts up a smoke screen and nobody will notice you've forgotten their names. Or if they do, they won't care anymore!

The Anecdotal Antidote: Storytelling as a Healing Technique

Introduction problems are one thing, but what about the really bad faux pas? How can you deal with that horrible, sinking terror that engulfs you right after one of those conversation-stopping social blunders, such as when the hostess overhears you telling someone that the only reason you came to her party was because you had nothing else to do? It's not easy to go on after one of these disasters until you do something to help heal the social wound you've inadvertently inflicted.

Keep in mind that everyone, at one time or another, makes a fool of himself while mingling. In fact, if you never made any mistakes, socially, you'd never improve your mingling skills. Taking risks, at least occasionally, is necessary to your mingling growth—I might even go so far as to say it is necessary to your social health. Because everyone knows what it feels like to make a faux pas, everyone is just as anxious as the one who has committed the social sin to see him recover. They want the tension to pass as much as he does. It is for this reason, I think, that Storytelling is such an effective way of mending the mingling faux pas.

The first thing you need for this technique is a really good faux pas story. The idea is to tell the witnesses of your current faux pas about something you did at another time that was *more* embarrassing than whatever it is you have just done. Ideally, it should be something that actually happened to you or to someone you know, because in the wake of whatever terrible social error you've committed, you have to be open and sincere in order to reestablish your position in the group. If told convincingly, your story will do much to dispel the humiliation surrounding you.

I confess I make faux pas often, especially while trying out new lines and maneuvers, but I have a great faux pas story—a true one—that almost always acts as a healing ointment for any mistakes I may have made. What I usually do, in the midst of the embarrassing silence or the nervous laughter I have caused, is to say something like, "I really can't believe I just did that [said that]. Boy, leave it to me! Did I ever tell you about the time I . . ." And I recount my Erica Jong story.

Years ago when I was looking for a job, someone had arranged for me to have an interview with Erica Jong, for the position of her secretarial assistant. At that time I was very nervous to be meeting a famous author, and it didn't help that I had broken my foot and was on crutches. On top of everything else, the evening of the interview it was raining and I couldn't get a cab. By the time I arrived at Ms. Jong's Upper East Side town house—my hair dripping wet, my crutches muddy—I was almost an hour late for the interview. I was a complete wreck. What a way to begin! But I took a deep breath and rang the doorbell.

The housekeeper let me in, and then the fabulous Erica Jong herself came sweeping down the front stairs. She graciously put out her hand.

"Hello, I'm Erica Jong," she said to me, smiling.

I looked straight into her eyes, smiled back at her, and said, "Hello, I'm Erica Jong."

(!)

In my nervousness and general disarray, I had actually introduced myself as *her*! There was a long, long moment of the loudest silence I have ever experienced—all three of us, I think, were totally confused—until Ms. Jong came through for both of us like the mingling pro she must be, and reminded me gently,

"You must be Jeanne Martinet."

"Uh . . . yes, that's who I am," I agreed sheepishly.

I don't think there are many moments (certainly I haven't had many) in life that can rival the embarrassment of the one I just described; however, the incident did end up serving a very useful purpose: *It gets me out of faux pas hot water almost every time.* After I tell that story, no one thinks too much about whatever current error I may have committed.

When using a personal anecdote as a healing tool, remember: It is better if you are the faux pas *perpetrator* in the tale you tell; it's not as effective to tell a story about someone else messing up. It can sound as if you are trying to compare your faux pas favorably to someone else's. (Although, if the story is outstanding in some way, it can work.) Also, you can use Storytelling to help someone *else* recover from a faux pas ("Hey, don't worry about it; let me tell you about the time I . . ."). This is the ultimate mingling move: In one fell swoop you've been kind to a fellow human being, endeared yourself to him or her for at least the remainder of the party, taken control of the conversation, and found a reason to tell one of your favorite stories!

Disclaimer: Storytelling won't work in every situation, of course. If you've just spilled hot coffee on someone's blouse, that person is probably not going to stick around while you tell a story.

All-Purpose Faux Pas Recovery Lines

If you don't have a good story to tell or if the faux pas isn't conducive to Storytelling, you may be able to use one of the recovery lines below to regain your balance. Also, these lines can be invaluable to the many people who are so paralyzed after a faux pas that a short sentence or two is all they are able to utter.

"Forgive me; I'm afraid I'm not feeling at all well. Especially not after that."

"Did I say that out loud?"

"Let's run that scene over."

"Okay. So I need some lessons in mingling. I'm an idiot."

"I'm on autopilot tonight, and I think I just crashed!"

"Excuse me. Another personality took over my body there for a minute."

"Um, is there a time machine anywhere around?"

"I'm terribly sorry, I'm afraid your beauty short-circuited me."

"Arrggh! Somebody up there must hate me!"

"I always wondered what would happen if I ever really embarrassed myself . . . I'm still alive. Good."

The Faux Pas–Moi: The Art of Denial

Sometimes the wisest course of action is to refute the crime. In the Faux Pas–Moi, the idea is to deny the very occurrence of the faux pas. It may seem like a dangerous ploy, but the pay-off can be big. And it is worth attempting when you are caught in truly horrible faux pas situations where the idea of trying to apologize or make excuses is not a palatable one.

There are four different ways to play out the Faux Pas–Moi:

- **Pretend you were misunderstood:** Suppose you commit a pretty bad faux pas, such as insulting a play or a book without realizing the person to whom you are waxing critical is the author. You have been chatting away in a group and the conversation turns to a play that recently opened, a play called *The Horrible Mistake,* and you say something like, "Oh, I saw that play; boy, it really dragged!"

    To your intense dismay the man to your right gives you an irritated look and says to you, "Oh really? I didn't think it dragged when I wrote it."

    Sudden disaster. Okay. Take a second to breathe. Remain calm. Do not allow your humiliation to show on your face. Instead, looked puzzled, and quickly think of the name of another play that is currently running.

    "So you're the author of *Mayhem on 42nd Street?*" you say. "Really? I thought a woman wrote that." Now, the playwright may be suspicious and suspect you are just trying to cover up your gaffe. However, the real trick to the successful Faux Pas–Moi is sticking to your denial position and refusing to cave in. Just say to yourself: Deny, deny, deny. It's like poker; you can't start to bluff and then change your mind halfway through the hand. (If you are not ready to go all the way with it, don't try this type of recovery at all.)

    At this point, the playwright will probably answer you dubiously with something like, "No, I wrote *The Horrible*

Mistake," as if to say, "Don't try to get out of it now," but re-member, you must not fold! Keep insisting, "But I was talking about *Mayhem on 42nd Street.* Isn't that what Joe was just talking about?" This is a great technique when it works; sometimes you can manage to totally erase the mis-take. The worst that can happen is that you "muff the bluff," and you are really not much worse off than you were before. After all, the injured playwright expects you to try to recover from such a blunder; the whole incident would probably be *more* insulting to him if you didn't make the effort. But hopefully he will believe your fervent denial. (His ego will want him to, in any case.)

- **Blame someone else.** This may seem unethical, especially if we are talking about blaming a push or a drink spill on another person present. (But don't rule it out. All's fair in love and embarrassment.) However, remember that you can of-ten blame an anonymous person. For example, in the case of the above playwright fiasco, you could try this:

  "Oh *no!* You're the playwright? Oh my gosh. You're not going to believe this now, I know, but I never even *saw* the play. I was just trying to contribute to the conversation. I heard some doofus on the bus talking about it. Boy, that's the last time I pretend someone else's opinion is mine."

- **Pretend you were only kidding.** Perhaps you are talking to a woman you haven't seen in a while. Fatigue or alcohol or boredom has made you careless, and you say to her some-thing like, "So, whatever happened to that weirdo you used to date?" The minute the words leave your lips you have a bad feeling. And sure enough, she answers with a cold smile, "I married him."

Here's what you do: Keep that smile on your face; laugh, if you can. Even slap the woman on the back for added effect, and say with appropriate merriment, "I know that! [Name of mutual friend at party] just told me. That was supposed to be a joke. So where is he tonight?" If the person still looks offended: "My mother always told me I shouldn't try to be funny."

- **Completely ignore it.** You have to be a cool customer to pull it off, but if you can do it, it's a no muss/no fuss way of effecting the Faux Pas–Moi. Here's what you do—or rather, what you don't do: Don't flinch, don't laugh, don't blush, don't acknowledge the faux pas in any way. Just erase it from your reality. It didn't happen. You didn't say it. You never did it. If you can act innocent enough, sometimes other people will begin to think they imagined the faux pas, or that at least whatever it was wasn't any big deal.

  This form of the Faux Pas–Moi is not just for daredevils; it is also for people who are too chicken or stunned to do anything about what has just taken place. Actually, the Faux Pas-Moi is sometimes the easiest, and maybe the only, dignified way to deal with what's happened.

  For example, one day a woman I know named Sally went to one of those terribly cute restaurants where the restrooms have confusing, arty symbols on them (often in the form of super-stylized hats or shoes), and so it was through no great fault of her own that she found herself suddenly . . . in the men's room. As soon as she entered, she saw a surprised (and occupied) man standing at a urinal. Sally felt that she had already come too far inside to leave gracefully. And so, un-ruffled, without blinking an eye, and ignoring the man's as-tonished stare, Sally quickly walked right up to one of the sinks, washed her hands, dried them with a paper towel, and walked back out. (She then proceeded to locate the ladies room, where there was—naturally!—a long waiting line.)

Admittedly, Sally's boldness is an extreme illustration of the Faux Pas–Moi, but it serves as a reminder that we must never underestimate the power we have at all times to create our own reality.

The Faux Pas-cifist

If there's one thing that warms my heart about the human race, it's watching a faux pas-cifist, or faux pas angel, at work. A faux pas-cifist is a witness, a bystander, or a third party who assesses a faux pas situation and steps in unselfishly to save the day. Of course, often the faux pas victim himself is kind enough to help the faux pas perpetrator over his embarrassment, but it's another thing altogether when an individual who would otherwise not be directly involved offers assistance. These people are no less than the heroes and heroines of the social universe.

A few years ago my friend Barbie and I were having a very intense tête-à-tête while standing in a crowd outside a lecture hall in Chelsea. Now, when you live in New York City you get used to discussing the intimate details of your life in the midst of strangers, because frankly, if you didn't you'd never talk anywhere but inside your apartment. You learn how to think of strangers both as people and as part of the scenery; you tend to ignore the fact that in this crowd twenty people could be listening to every word you say. Unfortunately, this practice can sometimes lead to trouble, and in this case caused me to forget one of the major rules of avoiding a faux pas—namely: *Be aware at all times of who is within earshot.*

I was filling Barbie in on a date I had had with a delicious guy who worked in the financial industry but also cooked and taught yoga. Just when I was saying, "Richard is really nice, seems really centered and healthy and all, except the one thing I can't figure out is that all his friends I met at this party we went to were so *incredibly* stuffy." I then happened to turn around and glance at the man behind me, who looked vaguely familiar and was, of course, none other than one of the incredibly stuffy friends in question. (Oh, when will I ever learn that New York City is just another small town?) There was no doubt in my mind that he had heard me; he was wearing a very hurt, angry expression and looked the other way when I looked at him.

When I realized that not only had I insulted this man but that he had also heard me gushing on and on about my date with his friend, I felt like knocking myself on the head until I was unconscious. I just sank into Barbie, closed my eyes, and put my head on her shoulder, too mortified to try to perform the Faux Pas–Moi or any other recovery technique. I felt completely and utterly doomed. The worst thing was that we were trapped in the crowd, so I couldn't even make a quick exit.

Luckily for me, however, the woman who was with the "stuffy man" suddenly stepped forward. "Excuse me," she said, tapping me on the shoulder. I had no alternative; I turned around. "I think I met you at the party on Saturday," she smiled and went on in a very composed manner. "I couldn't help overhearing what you were saying—you know, some of the people there are sort of stuffy until you get to know them better." She smiled again. Both the stuffy man and I hung on to her every word; she was our lifeline. She smiled even wider and said, "Richard *is* really nice, isn't he?" I blushed, but smiled back, gratefully. Then she indicated the stuffy man. "Did you meet Joe?" Blushing even deeper, I mumbled, "I don't think so." I introduced Barbie, and then this fabulous faux pas-cifist, whose name turned out to be Lila, led us all in a nice, four-way conversation. Joe was stiff at first, but I made sure I was especially nice to him and acted supremely interested in everything he said. By the time the crowd began moving back into the lecture hall I felt that Joe believed that I did not really think he was stuffy; and that he knew I was not a total grouthead and he was not going to run and tell Rich that I was one. Considering the enormity of the faux pas, it was a major, if not total, recovery, and I owed it all to Lila.

Lila was a master faux pas-cifist. There are not that many people who could and would handle the above situation with as much finesse and generosity. Most faux pas-cifists are lesser but still admirable people who might help others recover from faux pas using a simple recovery line. ("Don't mind Charley; he's a new parent—he's had about five seconds of sleep today.") I've seen a lot of people who have enough presence of mind to save another person from a common faux pas situation like an introduction problem. The faux pas-cifist simply takes over for someone who is floundering and fills in the missing name(s) or qualifiers. Another typical strategy of your garden variety faux pas-cifist is one of diversion; the kind interloper sees someone in trouble and fills the awkwardness with a change of subject or a witty comment.

All forms of faux pas-cifism are a godsend. I try to be a faux pas-cifist whenever possible and you should, too. With the kindness of strangers, as well as a bag full of recovery tricks, we will all be able to survive whatever the faux pas Fates throw at us.

NEGOTIATING TOUGH ROOMS

Every time you set out to go to a party, you are entering the world of the Unknown. It's important to be prepared for any scenario, to be ready to adapt the basic rules of mingling to fit, as you have no idea what may greet you once you get there.

The Sardine Can

Sometimes you are faced with what I like to call the Sardine Can. It's always best to try to arrive at a party on the early side. It's easier to talk to people before it gets crowded, and before separate cliques have had a chance to form and solidify. But let's say you arrive at a social function and discover it's wall-to-wall people. You hesitate at the door before going in; it seems like masochism to try to mingle in this teeming mass of humanity. You know that movement will be limited, fresh air scarce, and the line for the bathroom impossibly long. For some crazy reason, you go in anyway. (I know I always do.)

Once you've elected to become a sardine, here are some helpful tips on how best to proceed:

- **Use the most direct openings and simplest subject matter in your mingling portfolio.** Crowded parties are invariably loud, so any kind of complicated communication is out. Forget trying anything that entails irony or nuance, for example. People aren't going to be able to hear you. I recommend the Honest Approach as an entrance maneuver for the Sardine Can; people are more or less resigned to the fact that since they can't move, they have to talk to whomever happens to be next to them. For this reason, you'll find it easier than usual to get into conversations. It's just hard to have them in all the din!

- **Keep your eye out for anyone close to you who is making her way through the crowd.** This is your only hope of movement at a really packed party. If someone is strong enough or determined enough to wade through the multitude, take advantage of the path she is cutting and follow in her wake. You don't even have to know exactly where you are going; between the food, the bar, and the bathroom, you're bound to get closer to somewhere you want to be! This maneuver is much more extreme than Piggybacking; here, it's okay if you actually physically hang on to the person (as long as they don't mind). They probably won't even notice. When I see people doing this well, it reminds me of how city drivers use a speeding ambulance or fire engine to get through heavy traffic.

- **Don't worry about escape techniques.** While actual, physical movement may be limited, it's much easier to exit, psychologically speaking. The Sardine Can is a much more
  informal place, due to the decreased personal space. Rules of
  courtesy and etiquette are relaxed. Really crowded parties
  are so chaotic that people will hardly notice when you turn
  away from them. Even if you should happen to be in a one-
  on-one with an aggressive type who doesn't want to let you
  go, you won't lack for human sacrifices. Just reach out and
  grab someone, and hook him up with your bloodhound.
  Then . . . just Swivel! (see page 124).

- **Smile a lot.** Facial expressions of all kinds are at a premium
  while you are in the Sardine Can. Since hearing is limited,
  body language has to take the place of verbal communication. (In fact, a working knowledge of sign language could
  be a plus.)

The Thin Room

It's a whole different kettle of fish when you arrive at an
affair and find that there is practically no one there. It could be
that you're early, in which case it's only a temporary Thin
Room and you can wait it out. And as I mentioned earlier, being early can sort of "get you in on the ground floor" of the
party, which is a good thing. But if it's already an hour and a
half after the party's official starting time, those five or six guests
could be it. The rules of human kindness dictate that you remain, at least for a little while, since the hostess may be sui-
cidal at this point. (She's not about to let you get away in any
case; she's probably locked the door after you.)

Here are some suggestions about how to handle the Thin Room:

• **Encourage togetherness.** Probably the best time that can be had by all is if everyone stops trying to pretend it's a normal mingling situation. If there are only five people there, give up the structure of a cocktail party (where people are supposed to stand up and mingle) and help the hostess turn it into an intimate soirée instead (sit in chairs and on the sofa in a cozy circle). You should at least try to maneuver any separate groups closer together, for the simple reason that it is going to make it much easier for you to move between them. If you have a group of two people on one side of the room and a group of three way over on the other, it's going to be awkward to circulate. Having to walk by yourself across an empty room can make you self-conscious.

• **Offer to get people things.** The fewer people there are, the more energy is needed to create a fun atmosphere. Help the hostess by making sure the few guests who are there are as happy as they can be. Your ulterior motive: Volunteering to assist the host gives you more freedom to move around quickly. In the Thin Room it's essential that you not get stuck with one person for a long time—you could end up being the last two living souls at the party. The Thin Room can become the Empty Room in the blink of an eye.

• **Use Playing a Game as much as possible.** Game playing (see Chapter 3) can really help pep up a party. You should never, of course, suggest playing an actual party game like Charades or Dictionary without the express approval and encouragement of the hostess. (Although nothing saves a Thin Room so much as a good game of Twister!)

- **Bolster your hostess.** You may be disappointed that there aren't more people at the party, but just think how your hostess feels, if people she invited didn't show. Since you can't do anything about the fact that this is a Thin Room, take this opportunity to make your hostess feel good about her party. Flatter the food, praise the decorations, praise the gathering (the guests). In the Thin Room, it's vital that you project the positive. Everyone will appreciate it.

Mingling with Drunks

In almost every etiquette book ever written, from the early 1900s on, there is a section, usually written for the benefit of young ladies, on the proper and safe way to handle their inebriated gentlemen friends. In 1935, Alice-Leone Moats, in her famous *No Nice Girl Swears,* went so far as to categorize the different kinds of drunks: hilarious, lachrymose, loquacious, taciturn, argumentative, magisterial, belligerent, sentimental, amorous, and vomitous.

I rarely run into anything but the more benign type of drunk—the hilarious, the loquacious, the amorous, and the sentimental—all of them, depending on the level of inebriation, are easy to deal with. (Although I do know several people who fit into a separate category: the dangerously clumsy.) If you *do* happen to find yourself up against one of the more unpleasant species of drunks, here are some guidelines.

- **Never argue with a drunk.** It's useless. Humor the drunk, as you would a crazy person. But don't encourage him. If he says he is strong enough to lift you over his head, agree that he is certainly strong enough, but do not give him the opportunity to try it.

- **Never flirt with a drunk.** You may as well play with matches near an open tub of gasoline. This applies to women drunks as well as men.

- **Never tell a drunk you think he or she is drunk.** Unless he's your friend, and even then it's best to wait until morning to discuss the evils of overimbibing.

- **Remember that you don't have to mingle with a drunk unless you choose to.** It's the easiest thing in the world, usually, to escape from real drunks. Their senses are so dulled that you can use any escape technique you want and they'll never know what hit them. A lot of people seem to forget this and allow boring drunks to corner them for long periods of time. Don't buy into the drunk's illusion that he is in control mingling-wise (or any other wise). A simple "excuse me," and a hasty retreat is fine. Don't worry about leaving him standing all alone; he'll find someone else quickly enough. If you use the Human Sacrifice exit technique to escape from your drunk, try to find another drunk and sic them on each other. Otherwise, you could end up making enemies. Making enemies will not help you in mastering the art of mingling!

- **If the drunk is really offensive, you can use the experience to your advantage at the party.** Remember the Helpless Guest Ploy, where you asked people for help in order to have something to talk about? When you are being bothered by a heavy-duty drunk, you can have any number of people protecting you from the drunk, whether you are male or female. Don't forget the old Chinese proverb: Once someone saves your life, they are responsible for it forever. (Translation: Once someone saves you from a drunk, they've basically adopted you and will more than likely welcome you into whatever group they may be in later.)

- **Warn your host about a bad drunk.** By "bad drunk" I mean someone who is getting violent, or who is unsteady enough to damage property or chase away the other guests. "Live and let live" is a good philosophy, in most cases; after all, you are there to mingle, not to be a policeman. But it's nice to alert the host to a potential problem, so that he can decide whether or not he wants to do anything about it.

One last piece of advice on this subject: If there are a lot of besotted people at the party, cut your mingling short and go home. Or go straight to the bar and order a double martini.

Mingling with the Truly Arrogant

For nearly all of the many social situations one can imagine, my advice is to try to be as positive and friendly as possible. But when mingling with the Truly Arrogant, you will want to hold back a little on the warmth. This is not to say you still can't be charming, but if you are overly nice to arrogant people they will take it as a sign of weakness.

Truly Arrogant people usually travel in packs, so you'll probably have to deal with them in a group rather than just one here or there. They can be country club types, fashion designers, media people, or the very rich. But in any case, they are

hard to approach and often say things like, "What a lovely little thing that is you've got on, darling. I haven't seen anything
like that in ages!"

Of course, if you have any sense and you have the option,
you should just go home. Truly Arrogant people are no fun to
play with. But sometimes, for whatever reasons, you're forced
to stay and make the best of it. Perhaps it's a business party and
you're obligated to mingle; perhaps you're with a date and you
don't want to make her leave. But whatever the reason, it may
help if you remember a few simple rules for mingling with the
Truly Arrogant:

1. **Make use of the Survival Fantasies** (see page 11).
   If there is ever a time to use them, this is it. Mingling
   with the Truly Arrogant requires confidence.
2. **Breathe deeply.** This is always a good idea. It will
   help you to relax.
3. **Try not to flatter them.** Your first inclination will
   be to try to win them over by being nice. But Truly
   Arrogant people are usually super confident, and confident people don't really respect flattery. And flattery
   will give too much power to someone who is already
   assuming superiority.
4. **Tease the Truly Arrogant.** You have to try to
   communicate with them on their level first; show
   them you speak their language. Be careful, however.
   Your goal is bantering, not battering. This works best
   if you are dealing with the opposite sex. Tell him
   with a twinkle in your eye that you've heard some-

thing really terrible about him; or if he's a celebrity, pretend you've never heard of him (or confuse him with some other celebrity who doesn't look at all like him). You've got to be tough with these power mongers, and never let them see that it matters to you whether they like you or not.

However, once the Truly Arrogant person starts to warm up to you, once he begins to drop his snooty attitude, you must reward him by relenting and being nice to him. The rules for mingling with the Truly Arrogant apply only for as long as the person exhibits his arrogant behavior.

How to Crash a Party Without Breaking Anything

One of the toughest rooms to tackle is one where you don't officially belong. Attending an event to which you were not specifically invited is challenging, but sometimes it's worth it. Your demeanor and behavior should depend somewhat on what type of party "crashing" it is.

The self-invite (or prearranged) crash: Let's say you've heard from your good friend Ned that a mutual friend, Fiona, is having a big cocktail party. You don't know Fiona very well but you have met her and liked her. Ned, as a favor, might be willing to RSVP to Fiona and at the same time ask if he can bring you. Alternatively, you might email Fiona about something else and tell her you are hoping to see her soon, which is true, because what you are really hoping is that she will invite you to her party. Which, thankfully, she does.

You have to be an absolutely stellar guest when you have angled for an invite. As soon as you arrive, seek out the hostess, thank her for inviting you and tell her how glad you are to be there. Be extra careful not to eat and drink too much. Be an especially generous conversationalist. When people ask you, "So what's your connection to this party?" your answer should never be "I managed to get myself invited," but should be something like, "I don't know Fiona that well but she was kind enough to invite me. I was so pleased. I think she's marvelous!" Above all, praise the party every chance you get. Be helpful in any way you can, and make sure you are not the last guest to leave; you do not want to be conspicuously present. And be sure to send a thank-you note afterward.

The brazen crash. The brazen crash is when you dare to show up when you are both uninvited and unexpected. You've either tagged along with an invited guest at the last minute, or you know some of the people attending and you just decide to go on your own. The rules for mingling under these circumstances are the same as above. If, however, you are "outed" by the host ("Well hello! What are you doing here?") you may have to confess and throw yourself on his mercy "I'm so sorry, I didn't think you'd mind. I really wanted to reconnect with you." If it suits your personality and the host does not seem too unhappy about your presence, you could try a lighthearted, "I guess this makes me a party crasher!" In either case, if you get an icy reaction from the host, make a subtle but fairly hasty retreat from the party. Take time to say a pleasant good-bye to those people you have had nice conversations with, while making your way to the door.

The clandestine crash: If you've ever seen the movie *Wedding Crashers* you will know what I am talking about. Only true daredevils try this. If mingling were an official sport, this would come under the heading of Extreme. I've only done it when I was in my twenties and under the influence of a fearless adventure-seeker named Caleb. In these situations, you don't know the hostess, you don't know any of the guests. You just heard about the party somehow, or you have happened across it. There are two things you need besides as much information about the party and the guests as possible and an unbelievable amount of nerve. One is a killer outfit. You must be dressed impeccably and appropriately for the occasion. That way, even if the host or hostess (or bouncer) suspects you are a crasher, they may not care as long as you are a good addition to the party. Number two is a killer story; this is one of those techniques where you have to lie. You can't tell anyone you are crashing (unless you happen to meet another crasher). You are a secret agent, an interloper. I can't condone this kind of lying; I only believe in lying to save others' feelings. However, if you are going to be a real party crasher, you better bone up on your acting skills, and keep your story straight. The best stance is to be mysterious about your connection to the party. For example, "To tell the truth, I'm the ex of someone here at the party, but the person would rather I not reveal who she is." Of course, if you are confronted by the hostess, there is not much you can do, except try one of these do-or-die lines:

> *"No wonder I don't know anyone here! I'm so sorry, I thought this was Elizabeth Brown's party."*

"You got me. The truth is I'm writing an article [book/blog] on how to crash a party. I'd rather it not end with my getting thrown out."

THE SIT-DOWN MINGLE

Sit-down dinners, as pleasurable and socially complex as those occasions can be, do not, strictly speaking, fall under the category of mingling. What I'm talking about here are those times when you are at a large party and you make the fateful decision to sit down.

One evening I had a late party to go to after having been to dinner and a play. By the time I got to the party it was past eleven p.m. and I was tired. After greeting the host, I wandered out to a small terrace. I spotted an inviting empty chair, and without thinking, I sat down in it. It was one of those super slouchy chairs that seem to envelop you. *I'll just sit for a few minutes,* I thought.

Almost instantly I realized my mistake. The only other chair on the terrace was occupied by a blowsy woman who began talking at me nonstop about her Lhasa apso puppies. Where she got them, where she walked them, what she fed them, how much she loved them. Even how she dressed them. All attempts at subject changing—or at a back-and-forth conversation—failed. With a sinking heart I realized I had fallen right into the clutches of a human Venus flytrap. I was stuck. Now that I was already seated and the woman was talking to me so intently, it was going to be nearly impossible to get back up.

There are several reasons for sitting down at a party where most people are standing up. All evidence to the contrary, I am not a mingling nazi. Even I will agree that there are moments when you just need to take a break, and take a load off. Either your feet are tired (an excellent reason); you want to escape from someone, so you *pretend* your feet are tired; you've taken a plate of food from the buffet and are having trouble eating it while standing; or you would like to have a tête-à-tête with someone without being interrupted. All of these are very good reasons for sitting, but you should also be aware of the dangers.

The scariest thing about the Sit-Down Mingle is how difficult it can be to get back up. It is very hard to execute exit maneuvers from a seated position, should you find yourself Llasa-apsoed the way I was. Even if you sit down next to someone you know you'd love to talk to, that person could get up shortly after you've sat down, leaving you feeling awkwardly abandoned. Standing all alone at a party is not as conspicuous as sitting all alone at a party. You are taking a risk when you sit down, so make sure it's really where you want to be.

The other, more insidious danger is a purely psychological one: Once you are sitting down, you may lose your mingling momentum. You may find yourself thinking, "This is such a comfortable chair; maybe I'll just watch for the rest of the night. What's so great about talking to people anyway?" Warning: If you feel yourself slipping into this state of mingle-paralysis, get up! Immediately!

In order to master the Sit-Down Mingle, you have to learn how to get back on your feet. It's extremely hard to get free of someone (the Venus flytrap, for example) who is monologuing at you while you are both sitting down. She's basically got you where she wants you; you are her prisoner, or at least that's how it can feel to you.

Many of the normal escape techniques are problematic to perform from a sitting position; however, there are a couple that I have found work pretty well. The first is a version of the Buffet Bye-Bye and Other Handy Excuses (see page 83). But here, instead of saying "Pardon me, but I really must sit down," you interrupt and say, "I'm sorry, but I have *got* to stand up. If I don't get up now, I never will." In the more polite form of this you ask Venus if she would like to stand up with you. If she says yes, then once you have her on her feet, you can use the Human Sacrifice (page 92) or any number of other escape tactics to disengage.

The Human Sacrifice also can be done from a sitting-down position, in this manner: Find someone nearby and get his attention; wave him over if you have to. Try to bring him into the conversation a little; toss a few comments up at him; include him in whatever it is Venus is talking about. The minute the new person even smiles at something you or Venus says, start to get up, indicate your place, and say, "Would you care for a seat?" Depending on his aspect as you stand, you may want to use the more aggressive, "Would you save my seat for a second?" This is a bit wicked, because it's almost impossible for the new person to refuse, but as I've said before, all's fair in love and mingling. (Of course, you *don't* come back. In fact, try not to be visible to that side of the room for the rest of the evening.) The Human Sacrifice from a chair is definitely a bold move to make but at the worst, it's clunky.

One final word about the Sit-Down Mingle: Don't try it if you are extremely tired. There's only one thing I know of that's more impolite than getting drunk at a party and that's falling asleep. Especially if you snore.

QUICK FIXES FOR DIRE CIRCUMSTANCES

How to React to Unwelcome Physicalities

On occasion, someone will get physical with you in a way that makes you feel uncomfortable—a kiss on the hand, an arm around the waist, a pat on the head, a kiss on the back of the neck (once, someone even pulled on my ear, I swear)—and you are not going to know what to do or say.

Every person's sense of physical boundaries is different. Some people can accept a hug or a kiss from a perfect stranger, while others see this as an almost criminal invasion of their personal space. Hand kissing is considered the height of chivalry by some and the height of insolence by others. I myself don't really like hand kissing, especially when I have offered my hand for the purpose of shaking. It's like the greeting version of the bait and switch. *Wait, who said you could do that?* I always think.

When someone you don't know gets physical, it at least calls for some kind of comment. Whether you are flattered, embarrassed, or insulted, one of the lines below may come in handy. They are listed in order of most positive (That was very nice) to most negative (Try that again and I'll kill you). Deliver most of these with irony or at lease a twinkle.

"Why, thank you kindly, Sir [Madam]!"

"Chivalry is not dead!"

"I'm not that kind of girl!" (Use this even if you are a man)

"Must you do that?"

"Was that absolutely necessary?"

"Don't touch unless you're buying."

"Have you had your shots?"

"Excuse me, nobody informed me we had become intimate."

"Sorry, babe, you're on private property."

Handling Insults

The wildest story I ever heard about handling insults came from a friend of mine. I'll call him Nick (the name has been changed, for reasons that will be clear). It seems Nick was at a party where he was discussing a film he had just seen, when a man who had been listening suddenly challenged him.

"You don't really mean to say you *enjoyed* that piece of garbage?" the man said to him in a snide voice. Startled, Nick tried to defend himself.

"Well, . . . I mean it's not that I think it's great *art* or anything, but I thought it was entertaining, yes."

The man sneered. "Well, why would anybody in the film industry bother to make great art," the man said, "as long as there's pea-brains like you out there?"

Nick was absolutely stunned at the nastiness of this man, as were the other people within hearing distance. The insult had been so vicious, and so uncalled for, that Nick felt there was no way to respond to him—verbally, that is.

But Nick has his own method—a nonverbal one—of dealing with this kind of thing. He waited a little while, then located the drunkest person at the party and took him aside for a few minutes. Not too long after that, there was an unfortunate "accident." Nick had paid the drunk five dollars to spill his drink on the man who had insulted him!

Putting a contract out on someone at a party is never a good idea, and I am certainly not condoning it. Also, most insults are much less aggressive than the one Nick experienced. Most of the time you will just want to take the high road and walk away. However, you may have witnesses to the insult and feel the need to respond to keep the respect of the others around you. In this case, the best way to handle someone who has insulted you is to hit them immediately with a snappy comeback like the ones below. As you can see, they range from the corny (which can diffuse a tense situation) to the biting (which may be more satisfying to use). Warning: Make sure you have actually been insulted before using any of these lines. They are only for self-defense!

"I'd hate to have your nerve in a tooth."

"I think the rudeness police have a warrant out for your arrest."

"Are you this mean to everybody, or am I just lucky?"

"What charm school did you graduate from?"

"My mother always said I shouldn't talk to strangers; now I know why."

"Are you a good witch, or a bad witch?"

Cutting Your Losses (or, When to Just Give Up and Go Home)

The best poker players know when to fold. No matter how much skill you have or how much desire to play the game, sometimes it's simply not in the cards for you to mingle. Occasionally you can tell after only ten minutes that you should never have come to that particular function on that particular night. If you stay, you are going to end up having a bad time and, what's worse, it's going to be harmful to your self-image, because you are apt to mingle badly. So if you're too tired, too sick, or too distracted to put the right amount of energy into the experience of being at a party, accept this and act on it. In other words, cut your losses and go home.

Make very certain, however, that you are not throwing in the towel simply because you are *afraid* to mingle. Many people pose as introverts who can't be bothered with socializing when really it's because they're all frozen up with terror inside. Learning to recognize an onset of minglephobia is an important step in learning and mastering the art of mingling.

If you do decide to call it quits on a particularly ill-fated evening, don't let the experience prevent you from welcoming future mingling opportunities. Everybody skips a party now and then. But always remember that every new gathering, like every human being, is totally unique and unpredictable. You don't want to risk missing what might just turn out to be the best time you ever had.

8

The After-Party: Instructions for Following Up

Most of the time, or at least much of the time, you will find you have had a good time at the party. You will arrive home feeling proud and maybe even glowing inside, thinking how glad you are that you decided to go to the event. (I often find that it only takes one really fun conversation to make the party worthwhile.) Now you are recalling the great conversation you had with one or with several people you met. Should you let this feeling fade away along with the memory of the taste of the caviar canapés?

Whether it's prospective business contacts, potential friends, or a candidate for romance, it behooves you to try to pursue the people if you had such a good time talking to them. Will you be able to recapture the moment—the magic of the bonding, the laughter, the sense of kindred spirit you shared? Who knows? You certainly won't know until you try. One thing is for sure: Many long-term friendships begin with one good mingle.

HOW TO FOLLOW UP

The beauty of modern technology is that it is so much easier now to connect after a social event. In the Olden Days (by "Olden Days" I mean twenty years ago) we had no other choice but the phone, which even then was intrusive, because it puts the other person on the spot. It was also kind of scary for the caller, because of the possibility of a real-time, voice-to-voice rejection. Young people today have no idea of the terror that could be induced by the anticipation of having to leave an answering machine message you could not take back. It some cases, depending on why and who you were calling, it was like being asked to give a little impromptu speech in front of the person's whole family. Thank god for our electronic devices—among other things, they are invaluable for social first steps, for fostering new relationships. They allow us to make safe, casual overtures using exactly the right tone and method appropriate for the situation.

So which form of connecting should you use? Email? Facebook? It really depends on your age, and the age of the person you are contacting. It also depends on whether it's business or pleasure, as well as on what kind of information you exchanged with the person while you were at the party. For example, if you exchanged business cards, email may be your best choice, but if you exchanged cell phone info you are obviously going to be texting. Many people just hand their phone to the other person while they are talking, so they can put their contact information into their list of contacts. (This of course is a good sign for a future relationship.) Other people will write their emails on the back of the other person's business card. I know people who always initiate "first contact" by way of a Facebook message; other people I interviewed would never think of doing that.

Most people will either send an email, text, or connect on Facebook, Twitter, or LinkedIn. However, if you had a half-hour conversation with someone about how much you both love to post on a particular forum, by all means, connect with him there. Whatever your avenue of communication, don't be offended if it takes the other person a while to reply. People have vastly different social media and email habits. Some people check all their social media sites constantly, others only once every so often. Some people don't check their email for three days. Others check it every hour.

Here are a few quick tips on each of the major following-up modes:

Email or Text

Many people prefer email because it allows you to write a well-thought-out message, and it is less intrusive than sending a text. On the other hand, a lot of people use texting for everything and it can be a more casual way to say "Hi, glad to meet you." In either case, watch your use of emojis and emoticons until you know the person better. And don't include the new contact in a group message so that his information is visible to people he may not know.

Facebook

Some people love it, some people hate it. Facebook now has 1.23 billion users, so it is probably here to stay. The best thing it has going for it is that whoever you want to find is probably there. This is often the perfect venue to use a day or two after the party when you want to reach out to someone you met but you did not get their information and you can't quite recall their last name. If the person is a Facebook friend of the hostess, you can more than likely locate him by looking through the hostess's list of Friends. If you find the person, I recommend you send him a Facebook direct message, rather than a friend request (that could come later). To direct-message someone, go to their page and click on "Message." Do *not* post anything on their timeline unless you are sure they want all three hundred of their "Friends" to see it.

LinkedIn

LinkedIn is primarily a business networking site, a place where people present their professional profiles and make connections for career advancement or visibility. It is good for following up with someone you met in a business context. Keep in mind, however, that when you request that someone add you to their professional network on LinkedIn, it may take a long time for them to respond. Most people use that as a kind of résumé bulletin board, and are not actively engaging there. LinkedIn is probably the least invasive or aggressive way of connecting with someone because it does not imply a friendship in any way. You can send direct messages on LinkedIn, after you are connected to each other, but people usually do not get in touch that way socially.

Twitter

Twitter is much more public, and I happen to find it much easier and more straightforward in many ways than a lot of other sites. Because it is not about connecting as "friends" it can be an easier place to make a tentative connection with someone you have met who you either feel is out of your social sphere (so you don't feel comfortable emailing him or connecting on Facebook) or who you just want to keep an eye out for what he's up to. On one occasion I met a famous *New York Times* columnist with whom I had a very nice but brief conversation. The next day I followed him on Twitter. I was delighted when he followed me back, but I would not have been insulted had he not. Now, since we are connected, I could direct-message him (which I would do very sparingly) should I ever want to contact him for professional reasons.

Follow-Up Lines

Whether you choose to use Text, Email, Facebook, LinkedIn, Twitter, or messenger pigeon, here are some suggestions on how to word your follow-up.

Note: Don't expect to make a "date" right away. Your follow-up should just be to connect and let the person know they made an impression. If it's appropriate, remind him of the conversation you had either by making a reference to it or sending a picture or a link. If you had a funny exchange about a particular meme, it might be a nice way of following up to send the person a new link of that meme, something that he might not have seen yet. In a sense, you are continuing the conversation. You can even follow up with a link to those cat videos you really wanted to show him during the party (but you didn't because it would have been bad smartphone etiquette; see page 129).

Don't immediately ask the new contact to LIKE something of yours. Don't try to sell them anything right away. Go slowly and wait for a response back.

Here are some sample follow-up lines:

"That was such a great party. Loved meeting you and your husband. Let's keep in touch."

"Hello! I met you last night—we talked about being the only two who love licorice ice cream. It was lovely meeting you. Here's my website and email info. Hope to run into you again soon."

"Okay, you were right, I checked and it was Matt Dillon in that movie. Anyway, it was so nice meeting you. See you again I hope."

"Hi Bobby. It was great chatting with you last nite. I thought you might like to see the article I was referring to. Here's the link:_____ Say hi to Sue for me, and next time you are coming to the East Village please give me a call!"

Phonethics: When to Use Your Voice

It's amazing how quickly phone calls have become outmoded. These days most people will not even call their friends until they have mutually arranged a time beforehand. I know twenty-year-olds who never, ever check their voice mail. (They might see who has called them, but they won't listen to the actual message.) Because it is so unusual and the most intrusive way of reaching out other than showing up at the person's door, a phone call surprises, even irritates, when you call out of the blue.

But here's the thing: The voice is a hundred times more powerful than the written word. The sound of a voice evokes emotions and memory the way no text ever can. And there are some instances (rare, I admit) when a phone call at just the right time could completely cement the budding relationship.

Let's say you had an amazing conversation with a woman named Karen about your PEZ collection. You discovered at the party that you both have more than two hundred PEZ dispensers. You spent almost an hour talking to her and laughing about how weird it was to find another person who collects them. The next day, you are listening to the radio, and suddenly there is a segment on PEZ collections! You race to your purse, find Karen's card, and call her up immediately to tell her the program is on. This is a totally respectable reason for calling. By connecting by phone you have jumped up one level in intimacy. The sound of your voice is the best reminder of how much fun you had talking.

The Power and Glory of the Handwritten Note

Yes, as old-fashioned as hand-knit socks and butter churns, the handwritten note, be it postcard or letter, still occasionally works like nothing else. Snail mail can be effective when you are writing a thank-you or an apology, or if you want to make a certain kind of impression. It's such an anachronism that it can be a very powerful thing to do. It's as unusual as a singing telegram these days. It's thoughtful and generous, because it takes more time and trouble. If the conversation you had was one in a million, or the person did you a kindness somehow, why not show that you appreciated it? And always remember: Before following up with anyone new, you must be sure that your first communication is with your host or hostess to thank them for the party. If you can manage to send a handwritten note, it will usually score more points than you might imagine. Making other people feel good is one of your goals as a mingler.

GREAT EXPECTATIONS

It's important to temper your excitement with realistic expectations, after having met someone great while mingling at a party. We've all had it happen. If the conversation is warm and/or intellectually stimulating you can feel such a strong link to the person. You are certain that you've met a soul mate, you think it's a really special connection, whether platonic or romantic. It feels a little like finding a secret treasure. Especially if you went to the party with low expectations. Many times this connection will bear fruit; you will stay in touch, maybe get invited to a party at his house, or go for coffee or to a ball game. However, sometimes you find out it was just a mingling "one-night stand"; you are dismayed to realize after your email or text goes unanswered that he just didn't feel the same way about you.

This happens all the time, and you should not take it personally. It doesn't mean the other person did not have a fantastic time talking to you in the moment. It's just that for whatever reason—business, not enough in common, has too many friends already, wife won't approve—this person does not see it as anything other than one lovely conversation at a party.

Then again, some conversations are only one-offs for you and you have no desire or expectation to see the people ever again. This doesn't mean you didn't like them or that you did not value the mingle. But we don't always have time and energy to pursue a friendship with everyone we meet. If in fact it is you who sees it as a one-night stand, and the other person messages you, always be polite and return the text, email, or message. One quick "nice 2 meet u 2" is better than nothing. The unanswered email/text is simply unkind, even if you never plan to interact with the person again after that.

Some "mingles" blossom into relationships—business connections or friendships—others merely serve to enhance an evening. If you really want to keep things going, take things into your own hands. Become a host yourself. Throw your own party, and invite all those people you are hoping to see again!

While it's great making a connection that develops into a relationship, it's important to value mingling for mingling's sake. This should be your mingle mantra. All of those great conversations you have at parties, or while out in the world, really do help to enrich your life experience. Each interesting conversation becomes a small part of your social DNA forever, even long after you've forgotten it.

9

From Insecurity to Enlightenment: The Tao of Mingling

Throughout this book I have offered up countless practical techniques, ploys, strategies, tricks, and lines, and now that you've learned them all, I am going to ask you *not to think about them*. That's right: Don't worry about any of them. This may seem like a contradiction to everything I have been telling you. But like a painter who has mastered the use of color and all the brushstrokes, now you need to let your instincts take over. In spite of my previous detailed instruction, the best thing you can do to dispel your fears is to relax and be in the moment—to embrace the Tao of mingling.

"Tao" literally means "The Way." Taoists believe in the following essential paradox: The less worried you are about death, the longer you will live; the harder you try to do something, the less likely you are to do it. When we apply the philosophy of Taoism to the art of mingling, we might say that the more you try to control and think about all your social interactions, the harder they will be.

The main themes of Taoism are intuition, simplicity, spontaneity, and nature. Primary to the Taoist system is the idea of getting back to your essential state or true nature. So when your mother said "Just be yourself" it wasn't, after all, such bad advice—as long as she meant not just your true self but your *p'u* self. *P'u,* the Chinese term meaning "the uncarved block," signifies simplemindedness, or a simple beingness. A person who exemplifies the characteristic of *p'u* is one who looks at the world with wonder, without preconceptions; one who suspends judgment about everything. This person would never be worried that another person wouldn't like him. The idea of *p'u* is that things in their original state of simplicity contain their own natural power, and all the cleverness and wit in the world cannot equal the power of someone who is the pure embodiment of his inner nature.

Of course, it's one thing to talk about Taoism, it's quite another to really live it. But let's look at what some Taoist mingling practices might entail.

Wu Wei: Premingle Meditation

Let's say you've just moved to Boston. You've been invited to a party by the only person you know in your new hometown—a woman who was a college friend of your brother's. You are going to the party in hopes of getting to know some new people; however, you've never met the hostess before, much less any of the other people who are going to be there. You are therefore very nervous.

The Wu Wei meditation serves the same purpose as a survival fantasy, but here you are going to find the strength from within you rather than from the external world. You can do this meditation at home before you go to the party, in the cab en route to the party, in the elevator, or even while walking up the sidewalk to the front door (but not while driving, please!). It doesn't matter whether or not you've ever meditated before. Try to center yourself and focus on your breathing. Get very quiet and still inside. What you want to do is to get in touch with "the Great Nothing" and become an empty vessel.

Now, I'm not telling you to become empty-headed, or foolish. The principle of Wu Wei in Taoism is that of nonaction, or receptivity (otherwise known as "creative quietude," or "the art of letting-be"). The goal is to be in a place of complete receptivity when you enter the party. See yourself as a pool that is being drained of its water. That which is empty gets filled up; so if you are "empty," things—in this case, people—will flow to you. This doesn't mean that when you get to the party you'll stand motionless and stare with your mouth hanging open. Wu Wei does not mean inertia or laziness. It just means you are going to be entirely *present*. It is a sharpening of the mind, an undertaking to perceive the Tao within all things. Wu Wei is not inactivity, but a *readiness* for action. Don't try to remember any lines or techniques, just know they will all be there when you need them. Just be.

This isn't easy. It takes courage to trust in truly emptying your mind—it goes against what we have been taught about how to use our intellect. By doing this meditation, you should be able to at least partially stop your normal preparty internal dialog: "Now, what was that person's name who is giving the party? . . . Is my tie on right? . . . I wonder if there will be a lot of people . . . What am I going to say when I arrive? . . . I wonder if they'll have any scotch."

The Yin/Yang of Circulating

The yin/yang doctrine is based on the concept that everything in the Universe is in the process of becoming its opposite, that there are continuous transformations within the Tao. Life is always turning into death. Wet things are becoming dry, strong things are becoming weak. Remembering this will help you to stay fluid as you mingle, to accept the fact that everything is always moving and changing. In other words, you will be better at going with the flow.

Yang is usually seen as light, heat, male, sun, while yin connotes dark, cool, earth, female, moon. But I like to think of it this way: Yang is hello and yin is good-bye. With every hello you experience, there will be a good-bye. With every good-bye, a new hello.

If you fully grasp this cosmic truth about mingling, you will understand that all conversations are temporary. Your hello and good-bye already exist together, like yin and yang. Everything occurs in a cyclical motion; everything is continuous. (And no, I don't mean that the party will never end. This party will end, be it fun or tedious. And there will always be another one later on.) If everything is in the process of becoming its opposite, that means faux pas will soon be triumphs, awkward silences will become bons mots, minglephobia will become confidence, strangers will become friends.

The Art of Yielding: Using the Principles of Tai Chi (with Apologies to Tai Chi Practitioners)

I must apologize in advance to dedicated tai chi students who might be reading this, because what I am about to say is an oversimplification. Tai chi is a discipline that is based on going slowly, carefully, gradually; but for the purpose of this mingling technique I have had to condense many of its precepts.

Tai chi is a spiritual practice and martial art that uses the idea of softness, of being relaxed. One of the things my tai chi teacher used to tell the class was that we needed to "walk like a cat." In tai chi you strive for a cat's alertness and a cat's softness. You can spend weeks or years just learning to have your weight centered over the correct part of the feet. Interestingly enough (and though it is probably an etymological coincidence), *ming* means "the name" in Chinese; *ling* means "catlike alertness." It was this definition that first made me ponder the relationship between mingling and tai chi.

Much of learning to mingle well has to do with overcoming fear; similarly, the basis of tai chi chuan is to let go of tension in the body. Not only does relaxing release the tension, it is through relaxing that great strength and mastery comes. Hardness and resistance are the only real obstacles to success. The point is, whether you have just made a bad faux pas, or someone has been rude to you or just made an inappropriate pass, you will not be as negatively affected—or negatively affected at all—if you can employ this important yielding principle. When someone pushes, don't push back; be soft, yield; sink down into your center and *stay relaxed*. Go with the flow.

Let's say your Boston hostess turns out to be a less than enlightened person. When you get to the party she takes your coat, stares at you, and, in front of several other guests, says, "Boy, I can't believe you are so much shorter than your brother!" (In fact, your brother is six-foot-two and you are only five-foot-four.) Are you thrown off your game? You are not, because, having practiced being fluid and yielding, you bend like a tree in the wind. You smile, and say, "Actually, it's that my brother is so much taller than me."

In tai chi you also learn to "stick" to the other person, to follow their lead. You play with your opponent's energy. (In this vein, another, more playful response to the above comment might be a laughing "And I can't believe *you* are so direct!") Think of everyone you meet at the party as your teacher; jam with them, riff with them, dance with them. See how your music goes together. Feel where they are. But always stay centered in yourself.

How to Feel Happy When You Are Left Alone

Lao-tzu, the founder of Taoism, said, "Silence is a source of great strength." Taoism tells us to focus on the world around us in order to understand the inner harmonies of the universe. The Tao surrounds everyone, and we must listen to find enlightenment.

There you are, at the party of your brother's friend in Boston. Your hostess has pointed you toward the buffet; however, you see that the buffet is crowded and you don't feel like eating anything right away. You are standing alone in a sea of talking people. What should you do?

Nothing. You are fine. Everything is perfect. For the moment, absorb the energy of the party. If you don't know what to say, say nothing. If you don't know where to go, go nowhere. Taoists are in harmony with the way things really are because of being still and listening. Become one with your surroundings. Soon enough someone will be attracted to your energy and approach. Be prepared to let them in, to welcome the chi (the life energy) of the other person. But for right now, do not be afraid of *not* being in a conversation.

When we listen to music there is silence between the notes; it's a welcome silence because you know there is more music coming soon. You anticipate it with joy. The reason it is okay to be standing alone right now is that you know it's by choice, and it's temporary. In a sense, not talking to someone when you are at a party makes you appreciate it all the more when you *do* become engaged in conversation. Being content whether you are not talking or talking is how you become one with the party.

When you are really in the zone, when you feel so connected to the party that you get an actual buzzing feeling from it, you have attained what I call the Mingle Tingle. That's when you really get what the art of mingling is all about. Mingling can be a tool to understanding the Tao, and vice versa. All through this book I have been preaching to you about having a good time. I have tried to reinforce the idea that enjoyment is your only real goal. But actually there's a higher truth than that. Ultimately, mingling well with others is a way of getting in touch with all that is vibrant and wonderful about life.

So mingle on!

Index